I0428073

# BUDGET

The United States
Department of the Interior

# JUSTIFICATIONS

and Performance Information
Fiscal Year 2014

# OFFICE OF
# INSULAR AFFAIRS

References to the *2013 Full Yr. CR* signify annualized amounts appropriated in P.L. 112-175, the Continuing Appropriations Act. These amounts are the 2012 enacted numbers annualized through the end of FY 2013 with a 0.612 percent across-the-board increase for discretionary programs. Exceptions to this include Wildland Fire Management, which received an anomaly in the 2013 CR to fund annual operations at $726.5 million. The *2013 Full Yr. CR* does not incorporate reductions associated with the Presidential sequestration order issued in accordance with section 251A of the Balanced Budget and Emergency Deficit Control Act, as amended (BBEDCA), 2 U.S.C. 109a. This column is provided for reference only.

# Table of Contents

# General Statement

# I.   Bureau-Level Presentation

## General Statement

### 1. Introduction

The Office of Insular Affairs (OIA) carries out the Secretary's responsibilities for U.S.-affiliated insular areas. These include the territories of Guam, American Samoa, the U.S. Virgin Islands (USVI), and the Commonwealth of the Northern Mariana Islands (CNMI), as well as the three Freely Associated States (FAS): the Federated States of Micronesia (FSM), the Republic of the Marshall Islands (RMI), and the Republic of Palau.

The 2014 budget request is framed by long-term security interests of the United States in the western Pacific and Caribbean and serious economic and fiscal problems impacting the insular areas. Using General Technical Assistance funding, the Bureau of Economic Analysis (BEA) has successfully developed formal methodologies for measuring the gross domestic product (GDP) of the U.S. territories for the first time. The resulting GDP estimates released in July 2011 shed light on serious challenges faced in the territories and brought in to focus the vulnerability of their small undiversified economies. In the fall of 2012 BEA released estimates for GDP for 2010, and revised estimates for 2002 and 2009. The BEA for the first time also included estimates of GDP by industry, compensation by industry and consumer spending.

The economic picture painted by these GDP figures is reinforced by the U.S. Census Bureau's release of 2010 Census data for the territories. With the exception of Guam, all of the U.S. territories had population declines over the past decade led by the CNMI which experienced a 22.2 percent decline in population. These numbers provide clear evidence that islanders are leaving their homes to seek economic opportunity elsewhere. Population declines in the territories will likely compound economic woes as Federal formula grants based on population will decrease funding allotments to the territories. Financial assistance provided through the Office of Insular Affairs often fills gaps left by other Federal programs. As a result, the importance of the Office and the preservation of its financial assistance resources will be crucial to the insular areas as they work to turn around their struggling communities.

In the nine year time frame from 2002 to 2010 the estimates for American Samoa show that real GDP (GDP adjusted to remove price changes) decreased in 2005, 2008, and 2009 and increased in all other years. GDP increased 1.3 percent in 2010 after decreasing 3.1 percent in 2009. For comparison, real GDP for the U.S. (excluding the territories) increased 2.4 percent in 2010. The growth in the economy in 2010 largely reflected increases in territorial government spending and private fixed investment, including construction. Following the September 2009 earthquake and tsunami, the American Samoa Government significantly increased its spending, including hiring temporary workers for cleanup and recovery operations. Construction activity increased as homes and other structures damaged or destroyed by the natural disaster were repaired and rebuilt.

American Samoa's economic growth was tempered by a decline in exports of goods and services that was only partly offset by a decline in imports. Exports, which consisted overwhelmingly of exports of the tuna canning industry, were a major contributor to the decline in total exports in 2010. In 2009, one of the Territory's two canneries closed, significantly affecting economic growth. However, the canning industry continued to be a major private employer, while the territorial government continued to be the largest single employer. Recently adjusted per capita GDP figures show that American Samoa's low per capita real GDP was $9,315 in 2010. American Samoa's population declined 3.1 percent from 2000 to 2010, with its population at 55,519 in that year.

The six-year downward economic spiral in the Commonwealth of the Northern Mariana Islands was stopped in 2010 according to the new GDP data. The estimates for the CNMI show that real GDP, which decreased 19.8 percent in 2009 after decreasing 12.1 percent in 2008, grew at 2.3 percent in 2010. In addition, per capita real GDP for the CNMI increased in 2010, reflecting the growth in real GDP and a continued decline in the population.

The growth of the economy in 2010 largely reflected increases in territorial government spending, in consumer spending, and in exports of goods and services. Economic growth was tempered by an increase in imports. Exports increased for the first time after five consecutive years of decline. Tourism services, which make up the majority of exports of services, increased due to an increase in the number of visitors to the islands, offsetting continued declines in exports of goods.

For the CNMI, the GDP by industry estimates show that the distributive services sector (including retail and wholesale trade) and the territorial government were the largest contributors to overall GDP growth in 2010. Meanwhile, the manufacturing sector continued to contribute negatively to economic growth. The significant declines in manufacturing from 2005 to 2009 reflected the decline of the garment manufacturing industry. The compensation by industry estimates show trends in compensation for major industries. Total compensation grew in 2010, reflecting increases in both private and government compensation. However, compensation for the manufacturing sector continued to decline, falling each year from 2005 to 2010.

Per capita real GDP declined from $14,317 in 2007 to $11,484 in 2009. The CNMI's population decreased 22.2 percent from 2000 to 2010 to 53,883, as its foreign workers and citizens left the islands seeking economic opportunity elsewhere

Although challenging economic conditions are likely to persist in American Samoa and the CNMI, the outlook for Guam may be brighter. Guam's population grew 2.9 percent from 2000 to 2010 and is forecast to undergo expansion as the military relocates troops from Okinawa, Japan, to Guam. While some projects that lay the groundwork for the widely anticipated military relocation are underway, the scale of the relocation is not finalized. Further reductions in the scale of the military relocation would have a negative impact on projected economic activity on both Guam and throughout Micronesia.

The presence of thousands of U.S. military personnel presents economic opportunities for the island, but creates challenges on many fronts, including the creation of a strategy for needed civilian infrastructure upgrades.

GDP estimates for Guam show that real GDP increased 1.2 percent in 2010 after increasing 1.7 percent in 2009. The largest contributor to the growth in real GDP during this period was Federal government spending. The majority of this spending was by the Department of Defense. Federal spending increased in both 2009 and 2010; the increase in both years largely reflects increases in construction spending and in compensation. The tourism industry grew for the first time since 2004. Spending by tourists makes up the vast majority of Guam's exports of services.

After declining for two years, the more diverse economy of the U.S. Virgin Islands grew in 2010. The estimates for the U.S. Virgin Islands show that real GDP increased 2.9 percent. The trade balance contributed significantly to economic growth in 2010 as imports of goods declined more rapidly than exports of goods. As in previous years, the oil refining industry played a major role in the economy, accounting for the vast majority of imports and exports of goods. Figures in 2010 may represent the high point of the oil industry's contribution to the USVI economy. After 2012, the GDP will reflect the closure of Hovensa oil refinery in St. Croix, the loss of 2,000 jobs and a drop in imports and exports of petroleum products. This will have a serious impact on the local economy. The increase in GDP in 2010 also reflected increases in government spending and in private fixed investment, primarily construction.

For the U.S. Virgin Islands, the GDP by industry estimates show that services-producing industries were the primary source of overall GDP growth in 2010. Goods-producing industries continued to contribute negatively to economic growth. The decline in the goods-producing industries reflected the decline of the petroleum refining industry

The U.S. Virgin Islands and its relatively diversified insular economy experienced stable growth with real GDP growing at an average annual rate of 2.9 percent from 2002 to 2007. It had the highest real GDP per capita amongst the territories at $43,853 in 2010. Tourism accounts for almost all of exports of services, even as a significant decrease in the number of visitors adversely impacted tourist-related services.

The U.S. Virgin Islands has its own significant challenges including addressing consent decrees and EPA administrative orders to improve water, wastewater and solid waste facilities. The population of the territory declined by 2 percent from 2000 to 2010, and was 106,405 in the latest census.

Like American Samoa and the CNMI, the freely associated states of the FSM and the RMI are also suffering from a lack of economic growth. Since the introduction of the amended Compact in 2003, the FSM has experienced considerable volatility in economic activity, with GDP declining in three out of the initial six years. Overall GDP has declined by an annual average of 0.3 percent. Fiscal year 2010 turned out to be a good year for the FSM economy, reflected in continued expansion in construction as use of the Compact infrastructure sector grant picked up momentum, and a further injection of funds for Federal Aviation Administration (FAA) Airport Improvement Program projects. After several years of fiscal consolidation, 2010 saw a return to growth in public administration and the economy expanded by 2.5 percent overall. These trends continued to exert themselves in 2011 although good performance in fisheries replaced public administration as a source of growth, and the economy grew by 2.1 percent. Slow economic growth has been accompanied by outmigration to the U.S. Mainland and Guam. As a result of the decline or stagnation in incomes, outmigration as measured by net movements of air passengers leaving the FSM during 2004-10 has also been large. Clearly, there is a strong association between economic performance, employment prospects and outmigration.

The RMI's economy has performed more favorably in the last decade than that of the FSM's. However, economic performance in 2011 was lackluster with disappointing performance in the productive sectors of the economy. The contribution of fishing remained positive with a full year of operation of the new purse seiners commissioned in 2010; but, production at the loining plant was held back by labor shortages. Manufacturing output fell, reflecting lower international prices for coconut oil. Construction activity was also weak as the FAA road airport realignment project was held up due to environmental concerns. Output in education and heath expanded with recruitment of new teachers at the College of the Marshall Islands having a significant impact. Overall GDP grew by 0.8 percent. The generation of additional jobs has been insufficient to provide gainful employment opportunities for those seeking work, and outward migration remains substantial, averaging 1.7 percent annually during the amended Compact period.

Both the FSM and the RMI remain generally stable due to funding through the Compact of Free Association. This is partly due to documented improvements in financial accountability being demonstrated by all levels of government. However, the amount of funds available for government spending within the local economies is reduced annually as funds are shifted to deposits into the Compact trust funds. Without greater growth in their economies, neither government will be able to maintain the level of services to their populations in the medium term.

The migration of citizens of the FSM and RMI to the U.S. areas of Guam, Hawaii and the CNMI, has stressed the health and social service networks and education infrastructure in those areas. Combined data from the U.S. Census Bureau's (Census) 2005-2009 American Community Survey (ACS) and the required enumeration in 2008 estimate that a total of roughly 56,000 compact migrants from the FSM, the Marshall Islands, and Palau--nearly a quarter of all FAS citizens--were living in U.S. areas. Compact migrants resided throughout U.S. areas, with approximately 58 percent of all compact migrants living in the three jurisdictions. According to the 2008 required enumeration, compact migrant populations continued to grow in Guam and Hawaii and were roughly 12 percent of the population of Guam and 1 percent of the population of Hawaii. Each of these jurisdictions has reported that local costs for addressing the health, education, social service and law enforcement needs of the migrant communities far exceed the $30 million annually grant by OIA to help offset the costs.

The Office of Insular Affairs will continue to work with other Federal agencies, the affected jurisdictions and the FAS to better mitigate the impact of migration. OIA engaged the Census Bureau in 2013 to complete another enumeration of FAS emigrants in Hawaii, Guam, the CNMI and American Samoa. The results of this enumeration will direct allocations of Compact impact funds for the next five years beginning in 2014.

After the anticipated enactment in 2013 of the new financial assistance agreement between Palau and the U.S. achieved in 2012, the Republic of Palau will fully implement the new arrangements in 2014. The goals of the continued funding are to maintain the viability of Palau's trust fund and to keep government spending stable while Palau enacts policy reforms to strengthen its economy. Palau should see a spike in economic activity as it begins using capital improvement funding provided by the U.S.

Although each island's situation is unique, there are challenges they face in common. Each has very limited land and resources. Each has a small population and a limited pool of expertise to address the community's critical needs. Each is located in an area that is highly prone to destructive typhoons (cyclones, or hurricanes). Each faces constraints that mainland communities generally do not have, and they face those constraints in geographically isolated areas.

The Office of Insular Affairs strives to empower insular communities so they can overcome these challenges and seize upon opportunities as they arise. The Office will pursue strategies that foster economic development, lead to the adoption of sustainable energy solutions, promote sound financial management in the insular governments, and improve the quality of life for islanders while respecting and preserving their native cultures.

## 2. Budget Highlights

The proposed 2014 OIA budget is $687.7 million, an increase of $68,626 million and an increase of 4 FTE from the 2012 level.

### Total 2014 Budget Request
(Dollars in Thousands)

| Budget Authority | 2013 Full Yr. CR (PL 112-175) | 2012 Enacted | 2014 President's Budget | 2014 Change from 2012 |
|---|---|---|---|---|
| Current Discretionary | 63,882 | 63,494 | 64,310 | +816 |
| Current Mandatory | 40,867 | 40,867 | 27,720 | -13,147 |
| **Total Current** | **104,749** | 104,361 | 92,030 | -12,331 |
| **Permanent*** | **544,727** | 514,710 | 595,667 | +80,957 |
| **Total OIA** | **649,476** | 619,071 | 687,697 | +68,626 |
| *FTEs* | *41* | *37* | *41* | *+4* |

*Permanent funding in 2012 reflects actual amount.

OIA's budget is divided into two major categories of funding – current and permanent appropriations. Most of OIA's budget reflects mandatory commitments to U.S.-affiliated insular areas and is permanently appropriated. In 2014, these commitments include an estimated $314.6 million for fiscal payments to Guam and the U.S. Virgin Islands and $281.0 million for payments under the Compacts of Free Association. Current appropriations of $92.0 million are requested in 2014, a decrease of $12.3 million from the 2012 level. Most of this decrease is due to the temporary Palau Compact extension of $13.2 million not being proposed for 2014. The current appropriations request includes $64.3 million in discretionary funding and $27.7 million in mandatory funding.

**Palau Compact of Free Association**
On February 14, 2011, S. 343 was introduced in the Senate seeking to continue the U.S. Compact financial relationship with the Republic of Palau. Reaffirming the close partnership between the United States and the Republic of Palau, the bill represents a 15-year agreement that includes a $250 million package of assistance through 2024. Bill S. 343 has not been enacted by the U.S. Congress to date; and, OIA is not requesting current appropriations for Palau Compact assistance in 2014. However, the 2014 budget assumes enactment of the Bill and thus includes permanent appropriations of $66.4 million for the Palau Compact.

The Department of the Interior supports the President's Management Agenda to cut waste and implement a government that is more responsive and open. The Office of Insular Affairs budget supports the Department's plan to build upon the Accountable Government Initiative through a set of integrated enterprise reforms designed to support collaborative, evidence-based resource management decisions;

efficient Information Technology (IT) Transformation; optimized programs, business processes, and facilities; and a network of innovative cost controlling measures that leverage strategic workforce alignment to realize an effective 21$^{st}$ Century Interior organization.

Over the last three years, the Administration has implemented a series of management reforms to curb uncontrolled growth in contract spending, terminate poorly performing information technology projects, deploy state of the art fraud detection tools, focus agency leaders on achieving ambitious improvements in high-priority areas, and open government up to the public to increase accountability and accelerate innovation.

In November 2011, President Obama issued an Executive Order reinforcing these performance and management reforms and the achievement of efficiencies and cost-cutting across the government. This Executive Order identifies specific savings as part of the Administration's Campaign to Cut Waste to achieve a 20 percent reduction in administrative spending from 2010 to 2013 and sustain these savings in 2014. Each agency is directed to establish a plan to reduce the combined costs associated with travel, employee information technology devices, printing, executive fleet services, and extraneous promotional items and other areas.

The Department of the Interior is on target to reduce administrative spending by $217 million from 2010 levels by the end of 2013, and to sustain these savings in 2014. To meet this goal, the Department is leading efforts to reduce waste and create efficiencies by reviewing projected and actual administrative spending to allocate efficiency targets for Bureaus and Departmental Offices to achieve the 20 percent target. Additional details on the Campaign to Cut Waste can be found at http://www.whitehouse.gov/the-press-office/2011/11/09/executive-order-promoting-efficient-spending.

In support of the Administration's real property cost savings efforts, the Department issued a policy restricting the maximum amount of Bureau/Office-leased and GSA-provided space to FY 2010 levels and reducing the target utilization rate (sq. ft. per person) for office space by 10%. Through actions such as consolidations, collocations, and disposals, OIA plans to achieve a utilization rate of 250 usable sq. ft. per person by the end of FY 2014.

As part of the Administration's Management Priorities, the Department has initiated a plan for Information Technology (IT) Transformation designed to reduce spending by the consolidation of IT infrastructure and services under a single Chief Information Officer (CIO). The new IT shared services organization will transform the way that IT is delivered to over 70,000 DOI employees, using advances in technology to provide better services for less. OIA supports the Department's initiative to reduce 95 data centers by FY 2015 without disruption to mission.

Page intentionally blank

# Budget at a Glance

## B. Bureau-Level Tables

1.

| FY 2014 Budget at a Glance<br>Office of Insular Affairs<br>*(Dollars in Thousands)* | | | | | |
| --- | --- | --- | --- | --- | --- |
| | *2013 Full Yr. CR (PL 112-175)* | 2012 Enacted | Fixed Costs & Related Changes | Program Changes | 2014 Request |
| Assistance to Territories | | | | | |
| American Samoa Operations | 22,856 | 22,717 | 0 | +35 | 22,752 |
| Covenant Grants | 27,720 | 27,720 | 0 | 0 | 27,720 |
| Territorial Assistance | | | | | |
| Office of Insular Affairs | 9,523 | 9,465 | +474 | -491 | 9,448 |
| *Fixed Costs 2013* | | | [+45] | | |
| *Fixed Costs 2014* | | | [+429] | | |
| General Technical Assistance | 13,889 | 18,774 | 0 | -1,270 | 17,504 |
| *Compact Impact Disc.* | | [4,992] | | | |
| Maintenance Assistance | 2,251 | 2,237 | 0 | -1,156 | 1,081 |
| Brown Treesnake Control | 3,013 | 2,995 | 0 | +505 | 3,500 |
| Coral Reef Initiative | 1,004 | 998 | 0 | +2 | 1,000 |
| Water and Wastewater | 795 | 790 | 0 | -790 | 0 |
| Empowering Insular Communities | 2,218 | 2,205 | 0 | +766 | 2,971 |
| Compact Impact Disc. | 5,000 | 0 | 0 | +3,000 | 3,000 |
| **Total, Assistance to Territories** | 88,269 | 87,901 | +474 | +601 | 88,976 |
| | | | | | |
| Compact of Free Association - Current | | | | | |
| Federal Services | 2,831 | 2,814 | 0 | +4 | 2,818 |
| Enewetak | 502 | 499 | 0 | -263 | 236 |
| Palau Compact Extension | 13,147 | 13,147 | 0 | -13,147 | 0 |
| **Total, Compact of Free Association - Current** | 16,480 | 16,460 | 0 | -13,406 | 3,054 |
| | | | | | |
| **Total Current Discretionary/Mandatory** | 104,749 | 104,361 | +474 | -12,805 | 92,030 |
| Compact of Free Association | | | | | |
| Marshall Islands Compact | 68,090 | 66,839 | 0 | +8,407 | 75,246 |
| Federated States of Micronesia Compact | 106,663 | 104,984 | 0 | +4,045 | 109,029 |
| Palau Compact (Legislative Proposal) | 0 | 0 | 0 | +66,412 | 66,412 |
| *Federal Services Permanent* | | | | [+1,500] | |
| Compact Impact | 30,000 | 30,000 | 0 | 0 | 30,000 |
| Judicial Training | 347 | 340 | 0 | +13 | 353 |
| **Total Compact (Permanent)** | 205,100 | 202,163 | 0 | +78,877 | 281,040 |
| Fiscal Payments | | | | | |
| Guam Section 30 Income Taxes | 56,627 | 56,627 | 0 | 0 | 56,627 |
| VI Rum Excise Taxes | 283,000 | 255,920 | 0 | +2,080 | 258,000 |
| **Total, Fiscal Payments (Permanent)** | 339,627 | 312,547 | 0 | +2,080 | 314,627 |
| **Grand Total - Office of Insular Affairs** | 649,476 | 619,071 | +474 | +68,152 | 687,697 |

2.

**Office of Insular Affairs**
**2012 Funding (Budget Authority) by Activity and Insular Area**
**$(000)**

| Activity | Am Samoa | CNMI | Guam | USVI | FSM | RMI | Palau | Hawaii | DC | Other | Total |
|---|---|---|---|---|---|---|---|---|---|---|---|
| **Assistance to Territories** | | | | | | | | | | | |
| American Samoa Operations | 22,717 | | | | | | | | | | 22,717 |
| Covenant Grants | 10,089 | 9,523 | 6,086 | 2,022 | | | | | | | 27,720 |
| Office of Insular Affairs | 183 | 301 | | 130 | 80 | | 100 | 875 | 7,718 | 99 | 9,465 |
| General Technical Assistance | 2,906 | 4,032 | 3,006 | 3,132 | 390 | 2,008 | | 2,079 | | 1,221 | 18,774 |
| Maintenance Assistance | 295 | 585 | | 696 | 462 | 178 | | | | | 2,237 |
| Brown Treesnake Control | | 367 | 200 | | | | | 1,033 | | 1,395 | 2,995 |
| Coral Reef Initiative | 45 | 60 | 75 | 600 | 128 | | | | 90 | | 998 |
| Water and Wastewater | | | 790 | | | | | | | | 790 |
| Empowering Insular Communities | | | 2,205 | | | | | | | | 2,205 |
| *Total, Assistance to Territories* | 36,235 | 14,868 | 12,362 | 6,580 | 1,060 | 2,186 | 100 | 3,987 | 7,808 | 2,715 | 87,901 |
| **Compact of Free Association - Current** | | | | | | | | | | | |
| Federal Services | | | | | | | 500 | | | 2,314 | 2,814 |
| Palau Program Grant Assistance | | | | | | | 2,000 | | | | 2,000 |
| Enewetak | | | | | | 499 | | | | | 499 |
| Palau Compact Extension | | | | | | | 11,147 | | | | 11,147 |
| **Total Current Discretionary/Mandatory** | 36,235 | 14,868 | 12,362 | 6,580 | 1,060 | 2,685 | 13,747 | 3,987 | 7,808 | 5,029 | 104,361 |
| *Total, Compact of Free Association - Current* | 0 | 0 | 0 | 0 | 0 | 499 | 13,647 | 0 | 0 | 2,314 | 16,460 |
| **Compact of Free Association** | | | | | | | | | | | |
| Marshall Islands Compact | | | | | | 66,839 | | | | | 66,839 |
| Federated States of Micronesia Compact | | | | | 104,984 | | | | | | 104,984 |
| Palau Compact | | | | | | | | | | | 0 |
| Compact Impact | 14 | 1,930 | 16,827 | | | | | 11,229 | | | 30,000 |
| Judicial Training | | | | | | | | | | 340 | 340 |
| *Total, Compact (Permanent)* | 14 | 1,930 | 16,827 | 0 | 104,984 | 66,839 | 0 | 11,229 | 0 | 340 | 202,163 |
| **Fiscal Payments** | | | | | | | | | | | |
| Guam Section 30 Income Taxes | | | 56,627 | | | | | | | | 56,627 |
| VI Rum Excise Taxes | | | | 255,920 | | | | | | | 255,920 |
| *Total, Fiscal Payments (Permanent)* | 0 | 0 | 56,627 | 255,920 | 0 | 0 | 0 | 0 | 0 | 0 | 312,547 |
| **Total Permanent Mandatory** | 14 | 1,930 | 73,454 | 255,920 | 104,984 | 66,839 | 0 | 11,229 | 0 | 340 | 514,710 |
| **Grand Total - Office of Insular Affairs** | 36,249 | 16,798 | 85,816 | 262,500 | 106,044 | 69,524 | 13,747 | 15,216 | 7,808 | 5,369 | 619,071 |

3.

**Organization Chart**
**Office of Insular Affairs**

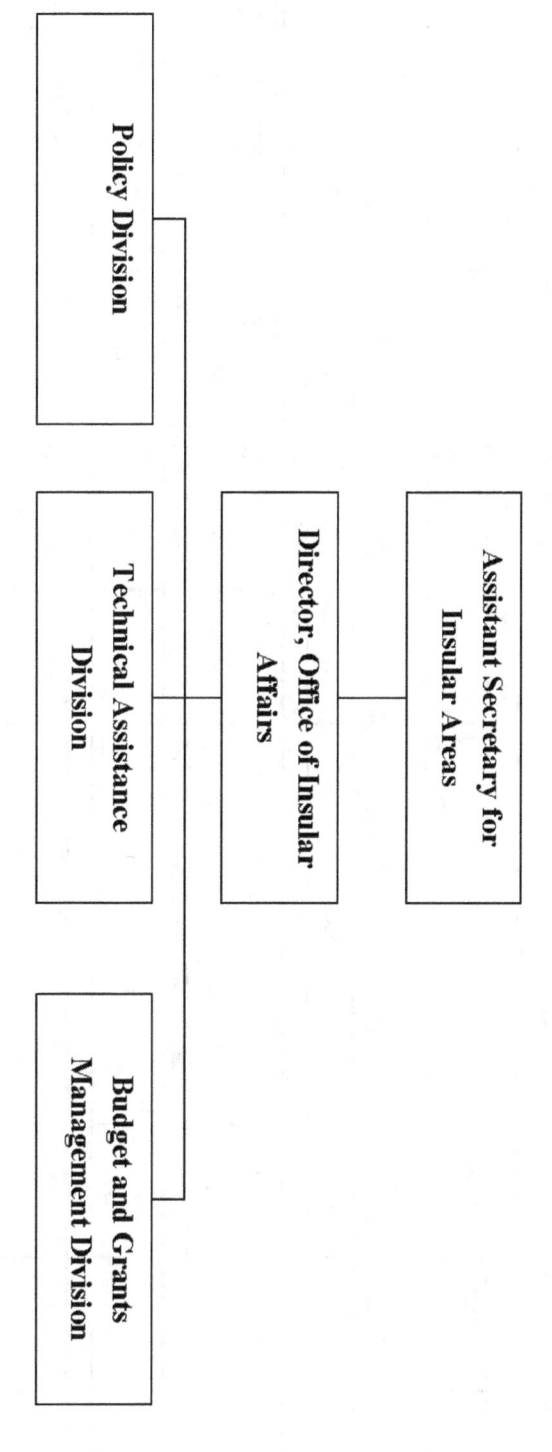

4.

## Mission Area 3: Advance Government-to-Government Relationships with Indian Nations and Honor Commitments to Insular Areas

### Goal #2: Empower Insular Communities

| Supporting Performance Measures | Type | 2009 Actual | 2010 Actual | 2011 Actual | 2012 Plan | 2012 Actual | 2013 Plan | 2014 Budget Request | Change from 2013 Plan to 2014 | Long-Term Target 2016 |
|---|---|---|---|---|---|---|---|---|---|---|
| **Strategy #1: Improve quality of life.** | | | | | | | | | | |
| 2075 Percent of Community Water Systems (CWS) that receive health-based violation notices from the US Environmental Protection Agency | A | 11 4% 17/149 | 18 1% 28/155 | 13 7% 20/146 | 10 4% | 17 5% 28/160 | 9 9% 16/161 | 9 9% 16/161 | 0 0% | 9% |
| Comments: | | | | | | | | | | |
| 2076 Change in the amount of petroleum used by utilities to deliver a megawatt of power | A | UNK | UNK | UNK | UNK | UNK | UNK | UNK | | Developing Baseline |
| Comments: OIA has a hired the National Renewable Energy Lab, through the Department of Energy, to develop the this metric. One year of data is available but percent change cannot yet be calculated | | | | | | | | | | |
| 2077 Percent of schools in acceptable condition based on specified safety and functionality standards | A | UNK | UNK | UNK | UNK | UNK | UNK | UNK | | Developing Baseline |
| Comments: OIA has hired the Army Corps of Engineers to develop this metric. Baseline assessments of all US territory schools should be completed in 18 months from June 2012 | | | | | | | | | | |
| Contributing Programs: Territorial Assistance, Covenant CIP, American Samoa Operations, Compact of Free Association | | | | | | | | | | |
| 2078 Number of patients requiring off-island medical referrals | A | 2676 | UNK | 1279 | 2606 | UNK | 2606 | 2600 | -6 | 2500 |
| Comments: 2 of the 4 territories have yet to submit 2012 medical referral reports. In 2012, American Samoa's hospital approved 231 cases to go off island but none were funded due to budgetary constraints | | | | | | | | | | |
| **Strategy #2: Create economic opportunity.** | | | | | | | | | | |
| 2079 Percent change in mean real GDP per capita | A | -7% | 2% | UNK | 0 8% | UNK | 0 8% (75 of 100) | 0 8% (75 of 100) | 0% (0 of 100) | 1 5% (1 5 of 100) |
| Comments: The Bureau of Economic Adjustment is expected to produce 2011 and 2012 estimates by Summer 2013 | | | | | | | | | | |
| **Priority Goal: Promote efficient and effective governance.** | | | | | | | | | | |
| 2080 Number of insular governments with on-time and unqualified single audits | A | 3 | 2 | 2 | 4 | 3 | 4 | 4 | 0 | 5 |
| Comments: The Governments of Guam, RMI and FSM National Government had on-time and unqualified single audits in 2012 | | | | | | | | | | |

# Summary of Requirements

# II. Account-Level Presentation

## A. Summary of Requirements

1.

OFFICE OF INSULAR AFFAIRS
ASSISTANCE TO TERRITORIES
2014 Summary of Requirements
*(Dollars in Thousands)*

| Activity/Subactivity | 2013 Full Yr. CR (PL 112-175) FTE | Amount | 2012 Enacted FTE | Amount | Fixed Costs & Related Changes FTE | Amount | Program Changes FTE | Amount | 2014 Request FTE | Amount | Change from 2012 (+/-) FTE | Amount |
|---|---|---|---|---|---|---|---|---|---|---|---|---|
| **ASSISTANCE TO TERRITORIES** | | | | | | | | | | | | |
| 1 American Samoa Operations | 2 | 22,856 | 2 | 22,717 | - | - | 4 | 35 | 2 | 22,752 | - | 35 |
| 2 Covenant Grants - Mandatory | | | | | | | | | | | | |
| Northern Mariana Islands Construction | - | 8,732 | - | 9,523 | - | - | - | (708) | - | 8,815 | - | (708) |
| American Samoa Construction | - | 9,964 | - | 10,089 | - | - | - | (42) | - | 10,047 | - | (42) |
| Guam Construction | - | 6,128 | - | 6,086 | - | - | - | (208) | - | 5,878 | - | (208) |
| Virgin Islands Construction | - | 2,896 | - | 2,022 | - | - | - | 958 | - | 2,980 | - | 958 |
| *Total, Covenant Grants* | - | 27,720 | - | 27,720 | - | - | - | - | - | 27,720 | - | - |
| 3 Territorial Assistance | | | | | | | | | | | | |
| Office of Insular Affairs | 38 | 9,523 | 34 | 9,465 | - | - | 4 | (491) | 38 | 9,448 | 4 | (17) |
| General Technical Assistance | 1 | 13,889 | 1 | 18,774 | - | 474 | - | (1,270) | 1 | 17,504 | - | (1,270) |
| *Compact Impact Disc.* | | | | *[4,992]* | | | | | | | | |
| Maintenance Assistance Fund | - | 2,251 | - | 2,237 | - | - | - | (1,156) | - | 1,081 | - | (1,156) |
| Brown Tree Snake Control | - | 3,013 | - | 2,995 | - | - | - | 505 | - | 3,500 | - | 505 |
| Coral Reef Initiative | - | 1,004 | - | 998 | - | - | - | 2 | - | 1,000 | - | 2 |
| Water and Wastewater Projects | - | 795 | - | 790 | - | - | - | (790) | - | - | - | (790) |
| Empowering Insular Communities | - | 2,218 | - | 2,205 | - | - | - | 766 | - | 2,971 | - | 766 |
| Compact Impact - Discretionary | - | 5,000 | - | - | - | - | - | 3,000 | - | 3,000 | - | 3,000 |
| *Total, Territorial Assistance* | 39 | 37,693 | 35 | 37,464 | - | 474 | - | 566 | 39 | 38,504 | 4 | 1,040 |
| **TOTAL, ASSISTANCE TO TERRITORIES** | 41 | 88,269 | 37 | 87,901 | - | 474 | 4 | 601 | 41 | 88,976 | 4 | 1,075 |

2.

OFFICE OF INSULAR AFFAIRS

COMPACT OF FREE ASSOCIATION - CURRENT APPROPRIATION

2014 Summary of Requirements

*(Dollars in Thousands)*

| | 2013 Full Yr. CR (PL 112-175) | | 2012 Enacted | | Fixed Costs & Related Changes | | Program Changes | | 2014 Request | | Change from 2012 (+/-) | |
|---|---|---|---|---|---|---|---|---|---|---|---|---|
| | FTE | Amount | FTE | Amount | FTE | Amount | FTE | Amount | FTE | Amount | FTE | Amount |
| **COMPACT OF FREE ASSOCIATION - CURRENT** | | | | | | | | | | | | |
| 1. Federal Services | - | 2,831 | - | 2,814 | - | - | - | 4 | - | 2,818 | - | 4 |
| 2. Enewetak | - | 502 | - | 499 | - | - | - | (263) | - | 236 | - | (263) |
| 3. Palau Compact Extension | - | 13,147 | - | 13,147 | - | - | - | (13,147) | - | - | - | (13,147) |
| **TOTAL, COMPACT - CURRENT** | - | 16,480 | - | 16,460 | - | - | - | (13,406) | - | 3,054 | - | (13,406) |

3.

**OFFICE OF INSULAR AFFAIRS**
**COMPACT OF FREE ASSOCIATION - PERMANENT APPROPRIATION**
**2014 Summary of Requirements**
*(Dollars in Thousands)*

| Activity/Subactivity | 2013 Full Yr. CR (PL 112-175) FTE | Amount | 2012 Enacted FTE | Amount | Fixed Costs and Related Changes FTE | Amount | Program Changes FTE | Amount | 2014 Request FTE | Amount | Change from 2012 (+/-) FTE | Amount |
|---|---|---|---|---|---|---|---|---|---|---|---|---|
| **COMPACT OF FREE ASSOCIATION - PERMANENT** | | | | | | | | | | | | |
| Assistance to the Marshall Islands: | - | | - | | - | | - | | - | | - | |
| Sector Grants | | 35,523 | | 35,881 | | 0 | | 2,022 | | 37,903 | | 2,022 |
| Audit | | 500 | | 0 | | 0 | | 500 | | 500 | | 500 |
| Trust Fund | | 13,307 | | 12,474 | | 0 | | 1,651 | | 14,125 | | 1,651 |
| Rongelap Resettlement | | 0 | | 0 | | 0 | | 0 | | 0 | | 0 |
| Kwajalein Lease Payment | | 17,256 | | 17,010 | | 0 | | 4,178 | | 21,188 | | 4,178 |
| Enewetak | | 1,504 | | 1,474 | | 0 | | 56 | | 1,530 | | 56 |
| Subtotal, Marshall Islands Assistance | - | 68,090 | - | 66,839 | - | 0 | - | 8,407 | - | 75,246 | - | 8,407 |
| Assistance to the Federated States of Micronesia (FSM) | | | | | | | | | | | | |
| Sector Grants | | 81,169 | | 81,397 | | 0 | | 765 | | 82,162 | | 765 |
| Trust Fund | | 24,994 | | 23,587 | | 0 | | 2,780 | | 26,367 | | 2,780 |
| Audit | | 500 | | 0 | | 0 | | 500 | | 500 | | 500 |
| Subtotal, FSM Assistance | - | 106,663 | - | 104,984 | - | 0 | - | 4,045 | - | 109,029 | - | 4,045 |
| Compact Impact | | 30,000 | | 30,000 | | 0 | | 0 | | 30,000 | | 0 |
| Judicial Training | | 347 | | 340 | | 0 | | 13 | | 353 | | 13 |
| Total FSM/Marshalls Compact (Permanent) | - | 205,100 | - | 202,163 | - | 0 | - | 12,465 | - | 214,628 | - | 12,465 |
| Assistance to the Republic of Palau | | | | | | | | | | | | |
| Section 211 (Government Operations) | | 0 | | 0 | | 0 | | 0 | | 0 | | 0 |
| Section 215 (Inflation Adjustment) | | 0 | | 0 | | 0 | | 0 | | 0 | | 0 |
| Palau Legislative Proposal* | | 0 | | 0 | | 0 | | 66,412 | | 66,412 | | 66,412 |
| Subtotal, Assistance to the Republic of Palau | - | 0 | - | 0 | - | 0 | - | 66,412 | - | 66,412 | - | 66,412 |
| **TOTAL, COMPACT, Permanent** | - | 205,100 | - | 202,163 | - | 0 | - | 78,877 | - | 281,040 | - | 78,877 |

*Assumes enactment of the amended Palau Compact in 2014.

4.

## SUMMARY OF REQUIREMENTS BY OBJECT CLASS
*(Dollars in thousands)*

| Appropriation: *Assistance to Territories* | 2012 Enacted | | Fixed Cost & Related Changes | | Program Changes | | 2014 Request | |
|---|---|---|---|---|---|---|---|---|
| | *FTE* | Amount | *FTE* | Amount | *FTE* | Amount | *FTE* | Amount |
| Object Class | | | | | | | | |
| 11.0 Personnel Compensation: | | | | | | | | |
| 11.1 Permanent positions - FTE-P | 37 | 4,316 | 0 | +55 | +4 | +350 | 41 | 4,721 |
| 11.5 Other personnel compensation | | 34 | | 0 | | +3 | | 37 |
| *Subtotal, Personnel Compensation* | *37* | *4,350* | *0* | *+55* | *+4* | *+353* | *41* | *4,758* |
| 12.1 Personnel benefits | | 1,205 | | +21 | | +98 | | 1,324 |
| 21.0 Travel & transportation of persons | | 572 | | 0 | | -146 | | 426 |
| 22.0 Transportation of things | | 106 | | 0 | | -106 | | 0 |
| 23.1 Rental payments to GSA | | 121 | | +51 | | 0 | | 172 |
| 23.2 Other rent, comm., and utilities | | 144 | | 0 | | -16 | | 128 |
| 24.0 Printing and reproduction | | 2 | | 0 | | 0 | | 2 |
| 25.0 Other services | | 6,598 | | +347 | | -4,421 | | 2,524 |
| 26.0 Supplies and materials | | 119 | | 0 | | -16 | | 103 |
| 31.0 Equipment | | 11 | | 0 | | 0 | | 11 |
| 41.0 Grants, subsidies & contributions | | 74,673 | | 0 | | +4,855 | | 79,528 |
| 99.0 Total requirements | 37 | 87,901 | 0 | +474 | +4 | +601 | 41 | 88,976 |

## B. Fixed Costs and Related Changes

### Office of Insular Affairs
#### Justification of Fixed Costs and Internal Realignments
*(Dollars In Thousands)*

| Other Fixed Cost Changes and Projections | 2012 Change | 2012 to 2014 Change |
|---|---|---|
| Change in Number of Paid Days | -18 | +15 |
| The combined fixed cost estimate includes an adjustment for one additional paid day between FY2012 and FY2013. The number of paid days do not change between FY2013 and FY2014. | | |
| Pay Raise | +49 | +40 |
| The PY column reflects the total pay raise changes as reflected in the the PY President's Budget. The BY Change column reflects the total pay raise changes between FY2012-FY2014. | | |
| Employer Share of Federal Health Benefit Plans | +32 | +21 |
| The change reflects expected increases in employer's share of Federal Health Benefit Plans. | | |
| Departmental Working Capital Fund | -137 | +347 |
| The change reflects expected changes in the charges for centrally billed Department services and other services through the Working Capital Fund. These charges are displayed in the Budget Justification for Department Management. | | |
| Worker's Compensation Payments | +0 | +0 |
| The adjustment is for changes in the costs of compensating injured employees and dependents of employees who suffer accidental deaths while on duty. Costs for the BY will reimburse the Department of Labor, Federal Employees Compensation Fund, pursuant to 5 U.S.C. 8147(b) as amended by Public Law 94-273. | | |
| Unemployment Compensation Payments | -1 | +0 |
| The adjustment is for projected changes in the costs of unemployment compensation claims to be paid to the Department of Labor, Federal Employees Compensation Account, in the Unemployment Trust Fund, pursuant to Public Law 96-499. | | |
| Rental Payments | +204 | +51 |
| The adjustment is for changes in the costs payable to General Services Administration (GSA) and others resulting from changes in rates for office and non-office space as estimated by GSA, as well as the rental costs of other currently occupied space. These costs include building security; in the case of GSA space, these are paid to Department of Homeland Security (DHS). Costs of mandatory office relocations, i.e. relocations in cases where due to external events there is no alternative but to vacate the currently occupied space, are also included. | | |
| Total, Fixed Costs OIA | +129 | +474 |

Page intentionally blank

# Language Citations

## C. Language Citations

### 1. Appropriation Changes

#### ASSISTANCE TO TERRITORIES

*For expenses necessary for assistance to territories under the jurisdiction of the Department of the Interior and other jurisdictions identified in section 104(e) of Public Law 108-188, $88,976,000, of which: (1)$79,528,000 shall remain available until expended for territorial assistance, including general technical assistance, maintenance assistance, disaster assistance, coral reef initiative activities, and brown tree snake control and research; grants to the judiciary in American Samoa for compensation and expenses, as authorized by law (48 U.S.C. 1661(c)); grants to the Government of American Samoa, in addition to current local revenues, for construction and support of governmental functions; grants to the Government of the Virgin Islands as authorized by law; grants to the Government of Guam, as authorized by law; and grants to the Government of the Northern Mariana Islands as authorized by law (Public Law 94-241; 90 Stat. 272); and (2)$9,448,000 shall be available until September 30, 2015, for salaries and expenses of the Office of Insular Affairs: Provided, That all financial transactions of the territorial and local governments herein provided for, including such transactions of all agencies or instrumentalities established or used by such governments, may be audited by the Government Accountability Office, at its discretion, in accordance with chapter 35 of title 31, United States Code: Provided further, That Northern Mariana Islands Covenant grant funding shall be provided according to those terms of the Agreement of the Special Representatives on Future United States Financial Assistance for the Northern Mariana Islands approved by Public Law 104-134: Provided further, That the funds for the program of operations and maintenance improvement are appropriated to institutionalize routine operations and maintenance improvement of capital infrastructure with territorial participation and cost sharing to be determined by the Secretary based on the grantee's commitment to timely maintenance of its capital assets: Provided further, That any appropriation for disaster assistance under this heading in this Act or previous appropriations Acts may be used as non-Federal matching funds for the purpose of hazard mitigation grants provided pursuant to section 404 of the Robert T. Stafford Disaster Relief and Emergency Assistance Act (42 U.S.C. 5170c).*

Note. - A full-year 2013 appropriation for this account was not enacted at the time the budget was prepared; therefore the budget assumes this account is operating under the Continuing Appropriations Resolution, 2013 (P.L. 112-175). The amounts included for 2013 reflect the annualized level provided by the continuing resolution.

#### COMPACT OF FREE ASSOCIATION

*For grants and necessary expenses, $3,054,000, to remain available until expended, as provided for in section 221(a)(2) of the Compact of Free Association for the Republic of Palau; and section 221(a)(2) of the Compacts of Free Association for the Government of the Republic of the Marshall Islands and the Federated States of Micronesia, as authorized by Public Law 99-658 and Public Law 108-188.*

Note. - A full-year 2013 appropriation for this account was not enacted at the time the budget was prepared; therefore the budget assumes this account is operating under the Continuing Appropriations

Resolution, 2013 (P.L. 112-175). The amounts included for 2013 reflect the annualized level provided by the continuing resolution.

**ADMINISTRATIVE PROVISIONS** (Including transfer of funds)

*At the request of the Governor of Guam, the Secretary may transfer discretionary funds or mandatory funds provided under section 104(e) of Public Law 108-188 and Public Law 104-134, that are allocated for Guam, to the Secretary of Agriculture for the subsidy cost of direct or guaranteed loans, plus not to exceed three percent of the amount of the subsidy transferred for the cost of loan administration, for the purposes authorized by the Rural Electrification Act of 1936 and section 306(a)(1) of the Consolidated Farm and Rural Development Act for construction and repair projects in Guam, and such funds shall remain available until expended: Provided, That such costs, including the cost of modifying such loans, shall be as defined in section 502 of the Congressional Budget Act of 1974: Provided further, That such loans or loan guarantees may be made without regard to the population of the area, credit elsewhere requirements, and restrictions on the types of eligible entities under the Rural Electrification Act of 1936 and section 306(a)(1) of the Consolidated Farm and Rural Development Act: Provided further, That any funds transferred to the Secretary of Agriculture shall be in addition to funds otherwise made available to make or guarantee loans under such authorities.*

*If the Secretary of the Interior determines that a territory has a substantial backlog of capital improvement program funds at the beginning of a fiscal year, the Secretary may withhold or redistribute that territory's capital improvement funds for the current fiscal year among the other eligible recipient territories. For purposes of this section, a territory with an expenditure rate of less than 50 percent shall be deemed to have a substantial backlog. The expenditure rate will be calculated on the last day of each fiscal year, currently September 30, and will be based on expenditures and receipts over the five most recent fiscal years.*

Note. - A full-year 2013 appropriation for this account was not enacted at the time the budget was prepared; therefore the budget assumes this account is operating under the Continuing Appropriations Resolution, 2013 (P.L. 112-175). The amounts included for 2013 reflect the annualized level provided by the continuing resolution.

## 2. Justification of Proposed Language Changes

Insertion: *If the Secretary of the Interior determines that a territory has a substantial backlog of capital improvement program funds at the beginning of a fiscal year, the Secretary may withhold or redistribute that territory's capital improvement funds for the current fiscal year among the other eligible recipient territories. For purposes of this section, a territory with an expenditure rate of less than 50 percent shall be deemed to have a substantial backlog. The expenditure rate will be calculated on the last day of each fiscal year, currently September 30, and will be based on expenditures and receipts over the five most recent fiscal years.*

The proposed insertion will allow OIA to more efficiently manage Capital Improvement Project funds (CIP). The CIP Program originates from Section 702 of Public Law 94-241, "The Covenant to Establish a Commonwealth of the Northern Mariana Islands in Political Union with the United States of America." The annually appropriated no-year funds ($27.72 million) are used to address a variety of infrastructure needs in the U.S. territories of Guam, American Samoa, the U.S. Virgin Islands and the Commonwealth of the Northern Mariana Islands through grants awarded by OIA. Though these are no-year funds, five year performance periods are assigned to the grants to encourage efficiency and to comply with Departmental regulations. At the end of the five years, any unspent funds are deobligated.

OIA has been advised by the Office of the Solicitor that because CIP funding is no year, once awarded it must remain with the recipient territory until expended unless Congressional approval to reallocate the funds is obtained. This requires OIA to return any unspent funds deobligated from a recipient's grant at the end of the five year performance period back to that recipient through future grants until the funds are fully expended.

This inability to redistribute deobligated funds among all four eligible U.S territories significantly reduces the effectiveness and efficiency of the CIP program by not providing incentive to the recipient to implement CIP-funded projects in a timely manner.

3. Authorizations

(1) <u>Guam</u>. Executive Order 10077, dated September 7, 1949, transferred administrative responsibilities for Guam from the Secretary of the Navy to the Secretary of the Interior. Executive Order 10137, of June 30, 1950, amended Executive Order 10077 to make the transfer effective on July 1, 1950. The Guam Organic Act was approved on August 1, 1950 (64 Stat. 384, 48 U.S.C. Sec. 1421 et. seq.) and declared Guam to be an unincorporated territory of the United States and provided that Guam's relationship with the Federal Government shall be under the general administrative supervision of the Secretary of the Interior. As a result of subsequent amendments to the Organic Act, Guam also elects its Governor and a Delegate to the United States Congress.

(2) <u>American Samoa</u>. In 1900, the islands were placed under the administration of the Secretary of the Navy by Executive Order. In the Act of February 20, 1929 (48 U.S.C. 1661), Congress stated that until it shall provide for the Government of the islands of American Samoa, "all civil, judicial, and military powers shall be vested in such manner as the President of the United States shall direct." The President vested these powers in the Secretary of the Interior by Executive Order 10264, dated June 29, 1951. Secretary's Order No. 2657, dated August 29, 1951, set forth the extent and nature of the authority of the Government of American Samoa and the manner in which the authority is to be exercised. Secretarial Order 3009 dated September 24, 1977, provided for an elected Governor and Lt. Governor for American Samoa, and elected officials first took office on January 3, 1978. Pursuant to Public Law 95-556, American Samoa, in November 1980, elected its first Delegate to the United States Congress.

(3) <u>U.S. Virgin Islands</u>. The islands were under the jurisdiction of the Navy Department from March 21, 1917, until March 18, 1931 (48 U.S.C. 1391), when responsibilities were transferred to the Secretary of the Interior pursuant to Executive Order 5566, dated February 27, 1931. Organic legislation was first passed in 1936 (49 Stat. 1812), and was revised by Public Law 83-517, effective July 22, 1954 (48 U.S.C. et. seq.). The latter has since been amended in various respects and the Virgin Islands' elected officials first took office on January 3, 1978.

(4) <u>Northern Mariana Islands</u>. On March 24, 1976, the President signed a joint resolution of Congress approving the "Covenant to Establish a Commonwealth of the Northern Mariana Islands in Political Union with the United States of America" (Public Law 94-241). The islands remained a part of the Trust Territory of the Pacific Islands under the jurisdiction of the Secretary of the Interior pursuant to Executive Order 11021 of May 7, 1962. Secretarial Order 2989, dated March 14, 1976, and effective January 9, 1978, provided for the separate administration of the Northern Mariana Islands, provided for the elected Government in the Northern Mariana Islands, and activated various sections of the Covenant. By Presidential Proclamation of November 3, 1986, and as a result of a valid act of self-determination pursuant to Section 1002 of the Covenant, the Northern Mariana Islands ceased to be bound by the United Nations Trusteeship Agreement of 1947, and became a commonwealth in political union and under the sovereignty of the United States.

(5) <u>Office of Insular Affairs</u>. Established August 4, 1995, by Secretarial Order No. 3191.

(6) <u>Covenant Grants.</u> Funding under the Northern Marianas Covenant was first established in 1976 under Public Law (P.L.) 94-241, A Joint Resolution to Approve the Covenant to Establish a Commonwealth of the Northern Mariana Islands in Political Union with the United States of America. This was later amended in 1986 by Section 10 of P.L. 99-396 (100 Stat. 840). These provisions were further amended by Public Law 104-134, enacted in 1996, which reduced annual funding to the Northern Mariana Islands and reallocated additional funding to other uses, including capital infrastructure projects in American Samoa, Guam, and the U.S. Virgin Islands.

(7) <u>Compacts of Free Association.</u> The Compact of Free Association Act of 1985 was enacted in January 1986 (P.L. 99-239) and authorized funding over a fifteen-year period for the Federated States of Micronesia and the Republic of the Marshall Islands. In December 2003, the President signed Public Law 108-188, enacting amendments to the Compact of Free Association and providing and additional twenty years of guaranteed annual assistance to the Federated States of Micronesia and the Republic of the Marshall Islands. The Compact of Free Association for the Republic of Palau was enacted on November 14, 1986 as P.L. 99-658, and was implemented on October 1, 1994. While the Compact of Free Association with the Republic of Palau was set to expire on September 30, 2009, P.L. 111-88 extended the terms of the Compact by one year.

These basic legal authorities have been supplemented and modified over the years by various omnibus territory acts and other program legislation.

Page Intentionally Blank

# American Samoa Operations

# III. Activity/Subactivity-Level Presentation

## A. American Samoa Operations

| Activity: | **American Samoa** | | | | | |
| Subactivity: | **American Samoa Operations** $(000) | | | | | |
| | | | **2014** | | | |
| | *2013 Full Yr. CR (PL 112-175)* | **2012 Enacted** | **Fixed Costs & Related Changes (+/-)** | **Program Changes (+/-)** | **Budget Request** | **Change from 2012 (+/-)** |
|---|---|---|---|---|---|---|
| General Operations | *21,963* | 21,863 | 0 | +34 | 21,897 | +34 |
| High Court | *893* | 854 | 0 | +1 | 855 | +1 |
| Total Requirements | *22,856* | 22,717 | **0** | +35 | 22,752 | +35 |
| FTE | *2* | 2 | 0 | 0 | 2 | 0 |

SUMMARY OF 2014 PROGRAM CHANGES

| **Request Component** | | |
|---|---|---|
| Program Changes | Amount | FTE |
| American Samoa Operations | +35 | 0 |

JUSTIFICATION OF 2014 PROGRAM CHANGES

The 2014 budget request for American Samoa Operations is $22.8 million, a program increase of $35,000 with no additional FTE from the 2012 level.

PROGRAM OVERVIEW

Each year the Office of Insular Affairs provides grant funds to American Samoa for the operation of the local government, including the judiciary. The American Samoa Government (ASG) does not have sufficient local revenues to fund the entire operating costs of its government. The purpose of this program activity is to fund the difference between budget needs and local revenues. The Department defines "budget needs" as the cost of maintaining current programs and services. Unless mutually agreed upon by the ASG and the Department, new programs are funded from local revenues.

A secondary objective of this program activity is to promote self-sufficiency. In this regard, the Department's policy is to maintain the operations grant at a constant level, thus requiring American Samoa to absorb the costs of inflation or costs associated with the growing population. Over the years, American Samoa has assumed an increasing percentage of the total costs of government operations. The American Samoa Operations funding provided currently represents approximately 18 percent of ASG's General Fund revenue and 18 percent of the LBJ Hospital's revenue.

*FY 2000 Tobacco Loan and Fiscal Reform Plan:* In response to a proposal from the American Samoa Government, Congress enacted legislation authorizing American Samoa to receive a direct Federal loan up to $18.6 million. The loan is to be repaid from ASG's share of the Tobacco Settlement Escrow Fund created for the purpose of paying debts ($14.3 million) and implementing financial reforms ($4.3 million). American Samoa identified a list of creditors who were willing to accept less than full dollar on the money they were owed. These creditors have now been paid. As a condition to the loan and requirement of the 1980 legislation, ASG submitted an Initial Fiscal Reform Plan on July 30, 2001. Subsequent to discussions and meetings between ASG and OIA, a Memorandum of Agreement (MOA) was signed by Governor Tauese P. Sunia and Deputy Assistant Secretary David B. Cohen on August 2, 2002. The MOA defined the implementation of the fiscal reform plan designed to bring the ASG annual operating expenses into balance with projected revenues for the years 2003 and beyond as required under Public Law 106-113 (H.R. 2466) Part 5, Section 125(b)(3). As authorized by the MOA, OIA released $4.3 million for expenses incurred by ASG under the Fiscal Reform Plan (FRP). The MOA requires ASG to submit quarterly reports, substantiated by an independent auditor, that provide updated revenue and expenditure information.

## 2014 PROGRAM PERFORMANCE

American Samoa plans to accomplish the following in 2014:

- Provide financial reports for quarter ending September 30, 2013.
- Provide financial reports for quarter ending December 31, 2013.
- Provide financial reports for quarter ending March 31, 2014.
- Provide financial reports for quarter ending June 30, 2014.

The following chart reflects the ASG's operations funding priorities for 2012, 2013 and 2014:

| Funding Category | 2012 Award | 2013 Proposed Award | 2014 Proposed Award |
|---|---|---|---|
| Basic (DOE/ASCC) Operations | $14,218,000 | $14,063,000 | $14,240,000 |
| LBJ Hospital Operations | $7,645,000 | $7,900,000 | $7,657,000 |
| High Court | $854,000 | $893,000 | $855,000 |
| Total | $22,717,000 | $22,856,000 | $22,752,000 |

*OIA Designated American Samoa as High Risk:* In an effort to improve accountability for Federal funds, OIA designated American Samoa as a "high-risk" grantee as provided for in 43 CFR 12.52, and as recommended by the General Accounting Office (GAO) and the Office of Inspector General (OIG). This designation allows OIA to require American Samoa grantees to comply with special conditions for future or existing grants. The special conditions may include: payment of grant funds on a reimbursable basis, withholding of approval to proceed from one project phase to another until receipt of acceptable evidence of current performance, additional project monitoring, and requiring the grantee to obtain technical or management assistance.

The "high-risk" designation will be removed once the ASG is in compliance with each of the following conditions: (a) the government shall have completed Single Audits by the statutory deadline for the two most recent consecutive years, resulting in opinions that are not disclaimed and do not contain qualifications that OIA determines in its reasonable discretion to be material; (b) the ASG shall have a balanced budget, as confirmed by independent auditors, for the two most recent consecutive years, without regard for nonrecurring windfalls such as insurance settlements; and (c) the ASG shall be in substantial compliance with the MOA and FRP.

Page intentionally blank

# Covenant CIP Grants

## B. Covenant CIP Grants Summary

| Activity: CNMI/Covenant Grants $(000) | | | | | | |
|---|---|---|---|---|---|---|
| SUMMARY TABLE | | | | | | |
| | | | 2014 | | | |
| | 2013 Full Yr. CR (PL 112-175) | 2012 Enacted | Fixed Costs & Related Changes (+/-) | Program Changes (+/-) | Budget Request | Change from 2012 (+/-) |
| CNMI Construction | 8,732 | 9,523 | 0 | -708 | 8,815 | -708 |
| American Samoa Construction | 9,964 | 10,089 | 0 | -42 | 10,047 | -42 |
| Guam Construction | 6,128 | 6,086 | 0 | -208 | 5,878 | -208 |
| Virgin Islands Construction | 2,896 | 2,022 | 0 | +958 | 2,980 | +958 |
| Totals | 27,720 | 27,720 | 0 | 0 | 27,720 | 0 |
| FTEs | 0 | 0 | 0 | 0 | 0 | 0 |

Covenant Capital Improvement Project (CIP) funds address a variety of infrastructure needs in the U.S. territories including critical infrastructure such as hospitals, schools, wastewater and solid waste systems. Improvements to critical infrastructure not only benefit the current population and businesses, but lay the groundwork to attract new investment to the territories thereby promoting economic development and self-sufficiency.

Beginning with 2005, OIA implemented a new competitive allocation system for the $27.72 million in mandatory Covenant CIP grants. It is based on a premise that all funds will be used for capital needs in the U.S. territories. This new process offers the U.S. insular area governments an opportunity to compete each year for a portion of the guaranteed funding in addition to other assistance or local funding that might be available. The territories are asked to submit capital improvement requests within a range of $2 million both above and below base (target) level funding.

Base level funding was established on the basis of historic trends in 2005 when the competitive allocation system was implemented. It was adjusted for 2012 based upon the performance of each of the U.S territories over the past five years as required by the 2004 Section 702 Funding Agreement between OIA and the CNMI.

FY 2012 Baseline Covenant Funding
($000)

| | |
|---|---|
| CNMI | 10,648 |
| American Samoa | 10,047 |
| Guam | 4,545 |
| U.S. Virgin Islands | 2,480 |
| TOTAL | 27,720 |

The determination of the annual allocation is made on the basis of a set of competitive criteria that measure the demonstrated ability of the governments to exercise prudent financial management practices and to meet Federal grant requirements. These criteria were revised in 2009 to strengthen these measures and to ensure that awarded funds are being utilized efficiently and effectively. In addition to the application of these criteria to the allocation of capital improvement assistance, the Office of Insular Affairs may consider the capacity of each insular government to absorb the amount of capital assistance it would otherwise qualify for and any special or extenuating conditions, such as unspent balances, that might require adjustments to the allocation. The competitive criteria are listed below:

Competitive Criteria for the Proposed Allocation of Mandatory Covenant CIP Funding

1. The extent to which the applicant is in compliance with completion deadlines established under the Single Audit Act of 1984.
2. The extent to which the applicant's financial statements were reliable.
3. The extent to which the applicant is exercising prudent financial management and is solvent.
4. The extent to which the applicant has demonstrated prompt and effective efforts to resolve questioned costs and internal control deficiencies identified in single audits.

5.  The extent to which the applicant has responded to recommendations identified in reviews completed by the Office of Inspector General, the Government Accountability Office and other Federal offices.

6.  The extent to which the applicant has demonstrated effective contract administration and compliance with local statutes and regulations regarding procurement practices and processes.

7.  The extent to which the applicant's capital improvement application is complete and submitted on time.

8.  The extent to which the applicant has complied with all reporting requirements applicable to past and ongoing grants in an accurate manner.

9.  The extent to which the applicant dedicates adequate resources to critical offices to help ensure properly functioning internal controls and efficient operations, including the presence of a qualified independent auditor with an adequately funded office and strong safeguards to its independence.

10. The extent to which the applicant is able to successfully expend capital improvement funds within the award period.

While the total available for funding stays constant ($27.72 million), allocations will vary from year to year depending upon the performance of each insular government with respect to the above competitive criteria. A change in an annual allotment does not necessarily indicate deterioration in performance. It instead recognizes those governments whose performance has increased during a fiscal year. For example, the 2014 request for Guam increased $1,333,000 over the baseline funding in the competitive process because it scored above the average of the insular areas on the ten criteria.

The competitive allocation system is applied to the $27.72 million in CIP funds using a point method. The territories are given a score on each of the above criteria. The criteria themselves are ranked so that those considered more significant would receive a higher weight than those considered less important in the overall, final score.

The following chart reflects the baseline distribution along with adjustments made to 2013 and 2014 requests based on each insular government's score on the competitive criteria.

Covenant CIP Grant Funding Levels
*Dollars in thousands (000's)*

| Territory | Baseline Funding | FY 2013 +/- Baseline | FY 2014 +/- Baseline | Total FY 2013 | Total FY 2014 | Diff +/- 2013 |
|---|---|---|---|---|---|---|
| CNMI | 10,648 | -1,916 | -1,833 | 8,732 | 8,815 | +83 |
| American Samoa | 10,047 | -83 | 0 | 9,964 | 10,047 | +83 |
| Guam | 4,545 | +1,583 | +1,333 | 6,128 | 5,878 | -250 |
| Virgin Islands | 2,480 | +416 | +500 | 2,896 | 2,980 | +84 |
| Total | 27,720 | 0 | 0 | 27,720 | 27,720 | 0 |

Covenant Capital Improvement Project funds address a variety of infrastructure needs in the U.S. territories including critical infrastructure such as hospitals, schools, wastewater and solid waste systems. The pie chart below displays 2012 spending of CIP by category. The expenditures in the chart also include Compact Impact funding spent on infrastructure projects.

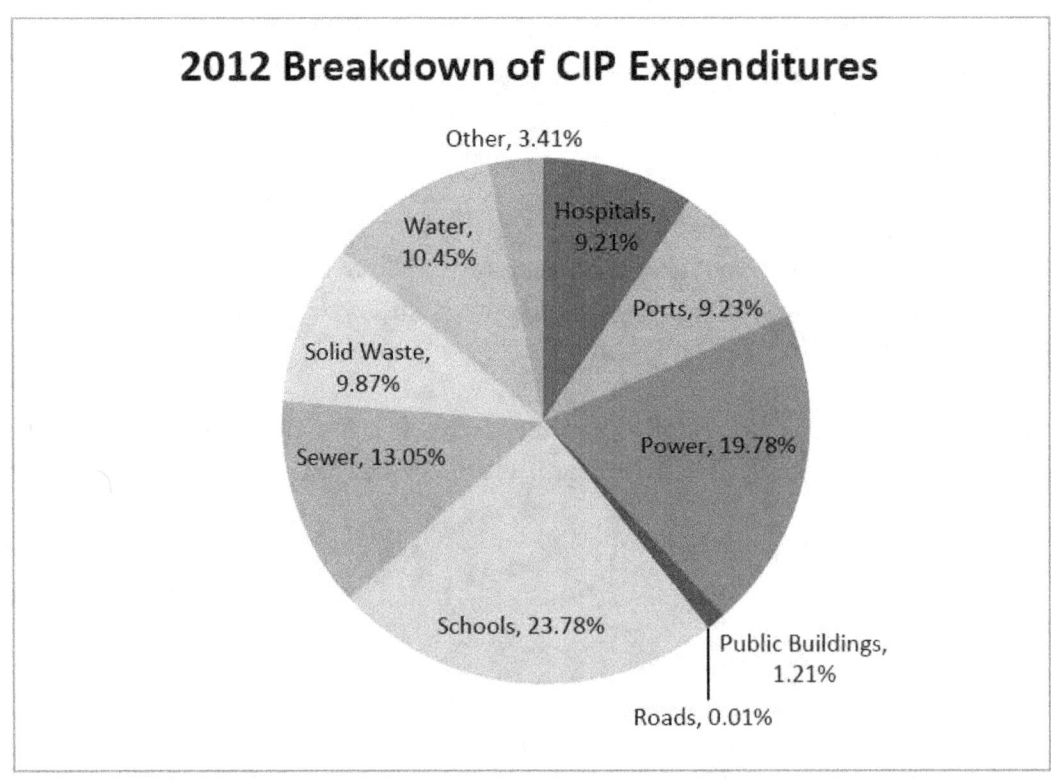

2012 Breakdown of CIP Expenditures

Other, 3.41%
Hospitals, 9.21%
Water, 10.45%
Ports, 9.23%
Solid Waste, 9.87%
Sewer, 13.05%
Power, 19.78%
Schools, 23.78%
Public Buildings, 1.21%
Roads, 0.01%

1.

| Activity: | CNMI/Covenant Grants | | | | | |
|---|---|---|---|---|---|---|
| Subactivity: | CNMI Construction   $(000) | | | | | |
| | | | **2014** | | | |
| | *2013 Full Yr. CR (PL 112-175)* | **2012 Enacted** | Fixed Costs & Related Changes (+/-) | Program Changes (+/-) | **Budget Request** | Change from 2012 (+/-) |
| | *8,732* | 9,523 | 0 | -708 | 8,815 | -708 |
| FTEs | *0* | 0 | 0 | 0 | 0 | 0 |

## SUMMARY OF 2014 PROGRAM CHANGES

| **Request Component** | | |
|---|---|---|
| Program Changes | Amount | FTE |
| CNMI Construction | -708 | 0 |

## JUSTIFICATION OF 2014 PROGRAM CHANGES

The 2014 budget request for CNMI Construction is $8.8 million, a program decrease of $708,000 with no change in FTE from the 2012 level. The budget request was calculated utilizing the CIP selection criteria and methods below. The process is further described in the beginning of this section (see Activity: CNMI/Covenant Grants summary section).

Beginning with 2005, OIA implemented a new competitive allocation system for the $27.72 million in mandatory Covenant CIP grants. It is based on a premise that all funds will be used for capital improvement needs in the U.S. territories. This new process offers the U.S. insular area governments an opportunity to compete each year for a portion of the guaranteed funding in addition to other assistance or local funding that might be available. The territories are asked to submit capital improvement requests within a range of $2 million both above and below base (target) level funding.

Base level funding was established on the basis of historic trends in 2005 when the competitive allocation system was implemented. It was adjusted for 2012 based upon the performance of each of the U.S territories over the past five years as required by the 2004 Section 702 Funding Agreement between OIA and the CNMI.

CNMI Baseline Funding........................ $10,648,000
Results from Competitive Process............. - $1,833,000
Programmed funding for 2014................ $ 8,815,000

## PROGRAM OVERVIEW

Section 701 of the Covenant (Public Law 94-241) states, *"The Government of the United States will assist the Government of the Northern Mariana Islands in its efforts to achieve a progressively higher standard of living for its people as part of the American economic community and to develop the economic resources needed to meet the financial responsibilities of local self-government."* Section 701 does not contain a finite standard to measure what is an adequate standard of living or the amount of economic resources necessary to meet the financial responsibilities of local self-government. Instead, it speaks of achieving progressively higher standards and a commitment by the Federal government to assist the CNMI in making progress.

The Federal government has granted more than $400 million in Covenant Capital Improvement Project (CIP) funding to the CNMI since the program started in 1978. The funding has been used for infrastructure improvements as required by Public Law 104-134. The U.S.-CNMI partnership in capital development has produced tangible results in terms of infrastructure improvements and the resulting economic development, which is especially significant when considering the CNMI's short history as part of the United States.

## 2014 PROGRAM PERFORMANCE

This past year saw substantial progress on several CIP-funded infrastructure projects in the CNMI. The Water Task Force completed the Papago Waterline Improvement Project which is intended to improve water delivery to the residents of the eastern portion of Saipan. The Commonwealth Utilities Corporation (CUC) completed the Agingan Wastewater Treatment Plant Rehabilitation. In addition, CUC completed several other CIP-funded projects intended to comply with Stipulated Order II, as required by the U.S. EPA and the U.S. Justice Department.

The requested $8.815 million for 2014 will be used to continue meeting critical infrastructure needs in the CNMI similar to previous years. Funds will be used for improvements to economic development, solid waste and education infrastructure. The proposed projects to be funded in 2014 are briefly explained below.

The CNMI has put an emphasis on developing solid waste infrastructure in recent years. In 2014, $2.1 million would be allocated towards the Puerto Rico Dump closure project mandated by EPA. In addition, $1.1 million each would be allocated to the Tinian and Rota Landfill projects which are intended to provide environmentally compliant solid waste disposal facilities for the islands' residents.

The Garapan Revitalization project would receive $2.0 million to continue drainage improvements in Saipan's largest village as well as to make visual enhancements intended to make it a more tourist friendly locale.

The CNMI has proposed that a football/soccer complex would receive $2.0 million for construction of a complex which would include several soccer fields, lighting, locker rooms, restrooms, bleachers, fencing and parking. The complex would promote sports education, interscholastic competition; as well as, enhance social services and physical well-being of the community.

Finally, $515,000 which would be used to address the routine maintenance needs of CNMI's infrastructure.

The following chart reflects the CNMI's funding priorities for 2012, 2013 and 2014:

| Funding Category | 2012 Award | 2013 Proposed Award | 2014 Proposed Award |
|---|---|---|---|
| Economic Development | $ 1,350,000 | | $ 2,000,000 |
| Solid Waste | $ 3,640,750 | $ 5,983,000 | $ 4,300,000 |
| Maintenance | | $    374,000 | $    515,000 |
| Water | $ 4,532,250 | $ 2,375,000 | |
| Education | | | $ 2,000,000 |
| **Total** | **$ 9,523,000** | **$ 8,732,000** | **$ 8,815,000** |

2.

| Activity: | CNMI/Covenant Grants | | | | | |
|---|---|---|---|---|---|---|
| Subactivity: | American Samoa Construction $(000) | | | | | |
| | | | 2014 | | | |
| | 2013 Full Yr. CR (PL 112-175) | 2012 Enacted | Fixed Costs & Related Changes (+/-) | Program Changes (+/-) | Budget Request | Change from 2012 (+/-) |
| | 9,964 | 10,089 | 0 | -42 | 10,047 | -42 |
| FTEs | 0 | 0 | 0 | 0 | 0 | 0 |

SUMMARY OF 2014 PROGRAM CHANGES

| Request Component | | |
|---|---|---|
| Program Changes | Amount | FTE |
| American Samoa Construction | -42 | 0 |

JUSTIFICATION OF 2014 PROGRAM CHANGES

The 2014 budget request for American Samoa Construction is $10.0 million, a program decrease of $42,000 with no change in FTE from the 2012 level.

Beginning with 2005, OIA implemented a new competitive allocation system for the $27.72 million in mandatory Covenant CIP grants. It is based on a premise that all funds will be used for capital improvement needs in the U.S. territories. This new process offers the U.S. insular area governments an opportunity to compete each year for a portion of the guaranteed funding in addition to other assistance or local funding that might be available. The territories are asked to submit capital improvement requests within a range of $2 million both above and below base (target) level funding.

Base level funding was established on the basis of historic trends in 2005 when the competitive allocation system was implemented. It was adjusted for 2012 based upon the performance of each of the U.S territories over the past five years as required by the 2004 Section 702 Funding Agreement between OIA and the CNMI.

American Samoa Baseline Funding........... $10,047,000

Results from competitive process............. $          0

Proposed funding for 2014.................... $10,047,000

The 2014 allocation for American Samoa was calculated utilizing the CIP selection criteria and methods discussed further in the beginning of this section (see Activity: CNMI/Covenant Grants Summary Table section).

## PROGRAM OVERVIEW

Until 1996, American Samoa received annual discretionary grants for capital improvement needs. These grants averaged approximately $5.0 million annually. During this time American Samoa fell further and further behind in keeping up with the infrastructure needs of a rapidly growing population. As a consequence, the people of the territory have been faced with increasing hardship and risk with regard to such basic needs as drinking water, medical services and education. In recognition of these severe problems, Congress enacted legislation in 1996 which directs a portion of the mandatory Covenant funds to be used to pay for critical infrastructure in American Samoa. The legislation required the development of a multi-year capital improvement plan. The plan was prepared by a committee appointed by the Governor of American Samoa. The Army Corps of Engineers served as technical advisors to the committee under an interagency agreement funded through the Office of Insular Affairs. This plan was transmitted to Congress on August 8, 1996. The Capital Improvement Master Plan is updated on an annual basis. All projects have been categorized into three general priority areas. First order priorities include health, safety, education, and utilities. Second order priorities include ports and roads. Third order priorities include industry, shoreline protection, parks and recreation and other government facilities. The objective of this program is to assist American Samoa in providing infrastructure to promote economic development and improve health, education and public safety.

## 2014 PROGRAM PERFORMANCE

Over the past year, several important Covenant CIP projects in American Samoa were substantially completed including the Lupelele, Matafao and Pavaiai Elementary School buildings, the renovation of the West Substation and the extension of the Tafuna Health Center. The LBJ Tropical Medical Center made steady progress on the design of the renovation of the dialysis unit and upgrading the electrical system while the American Samoa Power Authority continued connecting homes to the main sewer system in Tualauta.

In addition, the Department of Education made steady progress on the construction of two classroom buildings for the Leone High School while the Department of Public Works finished Phase B of the Petesa Happy Valley Village Road project.

The requested $10.1 million for 2014 will be used to continue meeting critical infrastructure needs in American Samoa similar to previous years. A total of $2 million of the 2014 request will be utilized to design and renovate the Intensive Care Unit at the LBJ Tropical Medical Center. The new facility will improve patient services and help the Medical Center meet life safety code requirements. An additional $1 million will help fund the construction of a multi-purpose building for the American Samoa Community College. The new 16,000 square feet building will house an auditorium and a student services center.

The $844,650 requested for Roads will be utilized to make improvements to Tafeta, Faleniu and Mapusaga Roads and to purchase needed heavy equipment for the Department of Public Works to provide proper maintenance for those roads.

Approximately $375,000 of the 2014 request will help fund the construction of a building at the over-crowded Male Correctional Facility. The new two-story building will have the capacity to accommodate 100 inmates allowing for greater security and maintenance with all convicted inmates housed in one building.

The 2014 request includes a total of $3.4 million to provide quality education for a growing population of students in American Samoa. About $1.6 million of the total will be used to build two classroom buildings at the Tafuna High School to alleviate overcrowding while $1 million will be used to construct a ten-classroom building at Pavaiai Elementary School. The remaining $800,000 will fund a new classroom building at Aua Elementary School. An additional $1 million will be used to purchase school buses to alleviate overcrowding.

The following chart reflects the ASG's funding priorities for 2012, 2013 and 2014:

| Funding Category | 2012 Award | 2013 Award | 2014 Proposed Award |
|---|---|---|---|
| Health | $4,639,900 | $7,044,650 | $2,000,000 |
| Education | $900,000 | - | $5,400,000 |
| Econ. Development | - | $1,000,000 | - |
| Water | - | - | $625,000 |
| Wastewater | $244,650 | - | - |
| Port | $2,300,000 | $300,000 | $300,000 |
| Public Safety | $1,500,000 | $921,150 | $375,000 |
| Roads | - | $200,000 | $844,650 |
| Parks | - | - | - |
| O&M Set-Aside | $504,450 | $498,200 | $502,350 |
| **Total** | **$10,089,000** | **$9,964,000** | **$10,047,000** |

**O&M Set-aside:** Five percent (5%) of all grant funds from the mandatory covenant account for American Samoa Construction is set aside for operations and maintenance. ASG provides a 100% match to all funds directed to O&M. This maintenance set-aside program requires specific plans from ASG for the use of the money as well as reporting procedures necessary to account for this fund.

3.

| | 2013 Full Yr. CR (PL 112-175) | 2012 Enacted | 2014 | | | Change from 2012 (+/-) |
|---|---|---|---|---|---|---|
| | | | Fixed Costs & Related Changes (+/-) | Program Changes (+/-) | Budget Request | |
| | 6,128 | 6,086 | 0 | -208 | 5,878 | -208 |
| FTEs | 0 | 0 | 0 | 0 | 0 | 0 |

**Activity:**  CNMI/Covenant Grants
**Subactivity:**  Guam Construction  $(000)

SUMMARY OF 2014 PROGRAM CHANGES

| Request Component | | |
|---|---|---|
| Program Changes | Amount | FTE |
| Guam Construction | -208 | 0 |

JUSTIFICATION OF 2014 PROGRAM CHANGES

The 2014 budget request for Guam Construction is $5.9 million, a program decrease of $208,000 with no change in FTE from the 2012 level. The request amount was calculated utilizing the CIP selection criteria and methods below. The process is further described in the beginning of this section (see Activity: CNMI/Covenant Grants summary section).

Beginning with 2005, OIA implemented a new competitive allocation system for the $27.72 million in mandatory Covenant CIP grants. It is based on a premise that all funds will be used for capital improvement needs in the U.S. territories. This new process offers the U.S. insular area governments an opportunity to compete each year for a portion of the guaranteed funding in addition to other assistance or local funding that might be available. The territories are asked to submit capital improvement requests within a range of $2 million both above and below base (target) level funding.

Base level funding was established on the basis of historic trends in FY 2005 when the competitive allocation system was implemented. It was adjusted for FY 2012 based upon the performance of each of the U.S territories over the past five years as required by the 2004 Section 702 Funding Agreement between OIA and the CNMI.

Guam Baseline Funding....................... $4,545,000
Results from competitive process............. + $1,333,000
Proposed funding for 2014.................... $5,878,000

## PROGRAM OVERVIEW

Legislation enacted in 1996 established a minimum six-year Covenant Capital Infrastructure Project (CIP) program for Guam as impact aid resulting from Micronesian immigration authorized in the Compacts of Free Association. Beginning in 2004 however, funding for impact aid for Guam is authorized and appropriated under the Compact of Free Association Amendments Act of 2003 (P.L. 108-188). Therefore, funds provided in 2005 and future years under this subactivity will be utilized for priority capital improvement projects in Guam and are in addition to Guam's allocated share of impact aid.

## 2014 PROGRAM PERFORMANCE

CIP-funded infrastructure projects on Guam made substantial progress this past year. The final phase of the Northern Region Community Pool Complex and Fitness Trail is nearing completion. Construction of the Central Guam Water Reservoir should be completed this year. In addition, work continues on the Gregorio D. Perez Marina Renovation project.

In 2014, Guam proposes to use its allocation of $5.8 million in CIP funding to address procurement of new school buses, infrastructure and a public safety communication system. The projects to be funded are briefly explained below.

The Department of Parks and Recreation and the Mayors' Council of Guam will allocate $1.3 million for renovations of park gymnasiums and recreational facilities. The continued replacement of the school bus fleet will require the procurement of 15 new buses totaling $2.5 million, including preventive maintenance. In addition, the Guam Police Department will allocate $2 million in its efforts to replace the outdated public safety communications system with a new AMSS/SmartNet System.

The chart below reflects Guam's funding priorities for 2012, 2013 and 2014:

| Funding Category | 2012 Award | 2013 Proposed Award | 2014 Proposed Award |
|---|---|---|---|
| Education | $2,652,000 | $2,063,000 | $2,545,000 |
| Port | $2,500,000 | | |
| Public Buildings | | $ 520,000 | |
| Public Safety | | | $2,000,000 |
| Water | $ 934,000 | | |
| Roads | | $2,000,000 | |
| Parks | | $1,000,000 | $1,333,000 |
| Maintenance | | $ 545,000 | |
| **Total** | **$6,086,000** | **$6,128,000** | **$5,878,000** |

4.

| Activity: | CNMI/Covenant Grants | | | | | |
|---|---|---|---|---|---|---|
| Subactivity: | Virgin Islands Construction   $(000) | | | | | |
| | | | 2014 | | | |
| | 2013 Full Yr. CR (PL 112-175) | 2012 Enacted | Fixed Costs & Related Changes (+/-) | Program Changes (+/-) | Budget Request | Change from 2012 (+/-) |
| | 2,896 | 2,022 | 0 | +958 | 2,980 | +958 |
| FTEs | 0 | 0 | 0 | 0 | 0 | 0 |

SUMMARY OF 2014 PROGRAM CHANGES

| Request Component | | |
|---|---|---|
| Program Changes | Amount | FTE |
| Virgin Islands Construction | +958 | 0 |

JUSTIFICATION OF 2014 PROGRAM CHANGES

The 2014 budget request for Virgin Islands Construction is $3.0 million, a program increase of $958,000 with no change in FTE from the 2012 level.

Beginning with 2005, OIA implemented a new competitive allocation system for the $27.72 million in mandatory Covenant CIP grants. It is based on a premise that all funds will be used for capital improvement needs in the U.S. territories. This new process offers the U.S. insular area governments an opportunity to compete each year for a portion of the guaranteed funding in addition to other assistance or local funding that might be available. The territories are asked to submit capital improvement requests within a range of $2 million both above and below base (target) level funding.

Base level funding was established on the basis of historic trends in 2005 when the competitive allocation system was implemented. It was adjusted for 2012 based upon the performance of each of the U.S territories over the past five years as required by the 2004 Section 702 Funding Agreement between OIA and the CNMI.

U.S. Virgin Islands Baseline Funding........ $2,480,000
Results from competitive process............. +$ 500,000
Proposed funding for 2013.................... $2,980,000

The 2014 allocation for the U.S. Virgin Islands was calculated utilizing the CIP selection criteria and methods which are discussed further in the beginning of this section (see Activity:  CNMI/Covenant Grants Summary Table section).

## PROGRAM OVERVIEW

Public Law 104-134, enacted in 1996, allowed Covenant funding, previous provided only to the CNMI, to be disbursed throughout the U.S.-affiliated insular areas.

Over the years each of the territories has received funding through this mandatory Covenant appropriation to fund Capital Improvement Projects (CIP).   While, in past years, American Samoa and the Commonwealth of the Northern Mariana Islands received set levels of funding, the U.S. Virgin Islands received irregular funding.   Recently though, the needs of the U.S. Virgin Islands have reached a threshold that without further addressing could pose a threat to the health and safety of residents and visitors.  Currently, the U.S. Virgin Islands is mandated to comply with consent decrees issued for various violations of Federal environmental laws.  Recent allocations of CIP funds have been utilized to assist the U.S. Virgin Islands in complying with these Federal mandates.

## 2014 PROGRAM PERFORMANCE

The 2010 and 2011 CIP grants are dedicated to address critical solid waste problems that the U.S. Environmental Protection Agency (EPA) has determined pose a serious threat to human health and the physical environment. There are two active landfills in the U.S. Virgin Islands: the Anguilla Landfill on St. Croix, and the Bovoni Landfill on St. Thomas. Both are unlined, lack leachate collection systems, and are sited within the coastal zone immediately adjacent to vibrant mangrove lagoons. Disposal of medical, septic, and small amounts of hazardous waste into these landfills has allowed the potential for leachate to contaminate ground water supplies and coastal waters and fisheries. In addition, both landfills have suffered from underground methane fires, as well as sporadic above-ground fires, which have raised public health concerns regarding the potential impact of landfill gas emissions and ash on air quality and on the widespread rain water collection systems in the adjacent area. The U.S. EPA has exercised strict scrutiny of solid waste operations in the U.S. Virgin Islands and has issued nine Orders for the two landfills. In order to comply with EPA's mandates, the U.S. Virgin Islands must bring into compliance and close the Anguilla Landfill and sections of the Bovoni Landfill. The closures must occur in full compliance with all applicable EPA and other governmental regulations.

The U.S. Virgin Islands plans to use the 2012 CIP grant to enhance the historic districts of Downtown Main Street on St. Thomas and the Christiansted Boardwalk on St. Croix. These projects which are part of a larger, integrated effort to revitalize the Virgin Islands community, will address a range of transportation and community needs for the local residents as well as the millions of visitors each year, most of who are from the U.S. mainland. The town of Charlotte Amalie on St. Thomas is one of the most intact historic commercial centers in this hemisphere while the Christiansted Boardwalk on St. Croix is the heart and soul of the downtown area. The revitalization efforts will build a better economic condition for businesses to compete more successfully as new commercial developments come along. The projects will not only improve the condition of the roadway and sidewalks, but will also improve the aesthetics and function of the street lighting making it safer and more inviting for pedestrians. The Government of the U.S. Virgin Islands seeks to develop the current infrastructure to improve the character, ambiance and economic vitality of its historic districts.

In 2013, the U.S. Virgin Islands proposes to use $1.48 million in CIP funds to continue the work of enhancing the historic district of Downtown Charlotte Amalie. In addition, $536,000 is dedicated to the restoration of Fort Christian to improve the appearance, functionality and stability of the seminal historic structure. The project intends to restore the fort to its historic 1790 period layout along the west, south, and east curtains and the historic 1874 period along the north curtain. The renovation work will allow for the reopening of the facility which is a major tourist attraction in Charlotte Amalie.

The U.S. Virgin Islands Water and Power Authority would receive $480,000 in 2013 to assist in the creation of a territory-wide Distribution Automation (DA) or "Smart Grid" system. The funding would be used to upgrade the currently installed pad-mounted and pole-mounted switches to more intelligent DA switches that will aid in improving system operation and reliability. DA is a proven technology that allows for the creation of a "Smart Grid" network that can perform effortlessly to isolate faulted lines and reroute power, thereby quickly restoring power to customers. This will eliminate the need to mobilize crews during emergency situations because the system can be accessed remotely. Overall, the Distribution Automation system will improve operational efficiencies and increase the performance to customers in a cost effective manner.

The Bureau of Correction's Golden Grove Adult Correctional Facility would receive $400,000 in CIP funds to install a control center equipped will all modern security, communication and life safety systems necessary for the controlling, housing and securing of inmates. The control center will be the central command post that will facilitate management, activation and monitoring all systems such as video, radio, fire alarm, emergency alarms, locking mechanisms, key control, restraining devices and vehicle distribution. The project will significantly improve the levels of security and control of the ever increasing number of inmates and detainees that require higher levels of safety and security.

In 2014, the U.S. Virgin Islands proposes to use $562,250 for the renovation and expansion of the clinic area of the St. Thomas East End Medical Center Corporation. The expansion is necessary to meet the current and anticipated increase in demands for primary, preventative clinical and dental services.

The Virgin Islands Bureau of Corrections would receive $465,000 in 2014 to refurbish the Anna's Hope Correctional Facility to house first time non-violent offenders. In addition, the Virgin Islands Bureau of Motor Vehicles would receive $52,250 in 2014 CIP funding for the reconstruction of the dilapidated inspection lane at the Bureau of Motor Vehicles on St. John.

The U.S. Virgin Islands proposes to use $500,000 in 2014 funding for upgrades at the Governor Juan F. Luis Hospital & Medical Center. The project will upgrade and enhance the Heating, Ventilation and Air Conditioning (HVAC) Heat Wheel in an effort to (1) improve the facility indoor air quality; (2) address patient safety and federal regulatory requirements; and (3) improve the facility energy conservation program.

An additional $500,500 will be used to upgrade the electrical system at the Roy Lester Schneider Hospital. The electrical system has not been updated since the hospital was built in 1982. The current aged utility transformers and generator have only a 12 percent capacity available, and the system is not able to efficiently carry the full operational needs of the building.

The Virgin Islands Department of Education proposes to use $400,000 in 2014 funding to repair leaky roofs at the Juanita Gardine and Pearl B. Larsen Elementary Schools.

The Virgin Islands Water and Power Authority (VIWAPA) proposes to use $500,000 in 2014 funding for a hazard mitigation plan to relocate critical overhead feeders underground in an electrical duct bank system in the downtown area of St. Croix. This project is part of the VIWAPA's effort to make the area safer for pedestrians by removing large transformer banks of poles and replacing them with pad mounted transformers. Additionally, VIWAPA will be removing all electrical lines which are currently dangerously close to buildings, allowing VIWAPA to correct the high voltage clearances in this area.

The following chart summarizes the U.S. Virgin Islands' funding priorities for 2012, 2013 and 2014:

| Funding Category | 2012 Award | 2013 Award | 2014 Proposed Award |
|---|---|---|---|
| Economic Development | $2,022,000 | $2,016,000 | - |
| Power | - | $480,000 | $500,000 |
| Public Safety | - | $400,000 | $465,000 |
| Health | - | - | $1,562,750 |
| Transportation | - | - | $52,250 |
| Education | - | - | $400,000 |
| Total | $2,022,000 | $2,896,000 | $2,980,000 |

# Territorial Assistance

## C. Territorial Assistance

| Activity:  Territorial Assistance   $(000) | | | | | | |
|---|---|---|---|---|---|---|
| **SUMMARY TABLE** | | | | | | |
| | | | **2014** | | | |
| | *2013 Full Yr. CR (PL 112-175)* | **2012 Enacted** | **Fixed Costs & Related Changes (+/-)** | **Program Changes (+/-)** | **Budget Request** | **Change From 2012 (+/-)** |
| Office of Insular Affairs | *9,523* | 9,465 | +474 | -491 | 9,448 | -17 |
| General Technical Assistance | *13,889* | 18,774* | 0 | -1,270 | 17,504 | -1,270 |
| Maintenance Assistance | *2,251* | 2,237 | 0 | -1,156 | 1,081 | -1,156 |
| Brown Tree Snake Control | *3,013* | 2,995 | 0 | +505 | 3,500 | +505 |
| Coral Reef Initiative | *1,004* | 998 | 0 | +2 | 1,000 | +2 |
| Water and Wastewater | *795* | 790 | 0 | -790 | 0 | -790 |
| Empowering Insular Communities | *2,218* | 2,205 | 0 | +766 | 2,971 | +766 |
| Compact Impact Disc. | *5,000* | 0 | 0 | +3,000 | 3,000 | +3,000 |
| **Total** | *37,693* | 37,464 | +474 | +566 | 38,504 | +1,040 |
| FTEs | *39* | 35 | 0 | +4 | 39 | +4 |

*Includes $4.992 million for Compact Impact

The Territorial Assistance activity involves funding for two major functions. The first is salaries and expenses of the Office of Insular Affairs. The Office has oversight responsibility for more than $600 million in annual financial assistance. Its policy and assistance activities involve dealing with virtually every major Federal agency, as well as seven insular governments. The Office has been able to attain clean audit opinions for all annual financial statements prepared under requirements defined in the Chief Financial Officers Act. Good financial management and effective internal controls are stressed within the

Office; however, in its report entitled "Opportunities Exist to Improve Interior's Grant Oversight and Reduce the Potential for Mismanagement" (GAO-10-347), GAO noted that OIA would be more effective with additional oversight resources.

The second major function within this program area includes the various technical assistance activities carried out by the office. OIA's technical assistance activities have always been considered its most effective tool to implement Administration policy, and to achieve mutually desired improvements in the insular areas. Many of the technical assistance activities are evolving from application-based grant programs, which reacted to problems identified, to programs that rely on the implementation of result-oriented plans. OIA asks the governments and assistance providers to form partnerships with us to identify major priorities and then develop and implement long-term action plans.

1.

| Activity: | Territorial Assistance | | | | | |
| Subactivity: | Office of Insular Affairs (OIA) $(000) | | | | | |
| | | | 2014 | | | |
| | 2013 Full Yr. CR (PL 112-175) | 2012 Enacted | Fixed Costs & Related Changes (+/-) | Program Changes (+/-) | Budget Request | Change from 2012 (+/-) |
| | 9,523 | 9,465 | +474 | -491 | 9,448 | -17 |
| FTEs | 38 | 34 | 0 | +4 | 38 | +4 |

## SUMMARY OF 2014 PROGRAM CHANGES

| Request Component | | |
|---|---|---|
| Program Changes | Amount | FTE |
| Office of Insular Affairs | -491 | +4 |

## JUSTIFICATION OF 2014 PROGRAM CHANGES

The 2014 budget request for the Office of Insular Affairs (OIA) is $9.4 million and 38 FTE, a net decrease of $17,000 and an increase of 4 FTE from the 2012 level. The 2014 budget request for the Office of Insular Affairs includes $474,000 for fixed costs and related changes as well as a general program decrease of $491,000. OIA is currently in the process of filling critical vacancies which suppressed the 2012 actual FTE level. Both OIG and GAO reports have stressed that the Office of Insular Affairs needs additional resources to provide adequate oversight for the Office's financial assistance resources.

## PROGRAM OVERVIEW

The Office of Insular Affairs carries out the Secretary's responsibilities with respect to U.S.-affiliated insular areas. The office is organized into three divisions:

1.) The Policy Division: performs general program, political, and economic analysis. It monitors and tracks Federal programs extended to the insular areas and handles legislative affairs, other than those related to the appropriations process. The Division maintains a field presence in the U.S. Virgin Islands and American Samoa.

2.) The Technical Assistance Division: manages all General Technical Assistance grants and cooperative agreements which provide support not otherwise available to the insular areas to combat deteriorating economic and fiscal conditions. Activities often include, but are not limited to, building institutional capacity in the following critical areas: health care, education, public safety, data collection and analysis, fiscal accountability, energy, transportation, economic development and communication. The division also manages the Brown Treesnake and Maintenance Assistance programs as well as payments to the U.S. Virgin Islands (rum excise taxes) and Guam (Section 30 income taxes).

3.) The Budget and Grants Management Division: is responsible for budget formulation and presentation, chief financial officer activities, and performance planning. It manages financial assistance under the Compacts of Free Association, operations and capital improvement grants to U.S. territories, Compact Impact grants, and infrastructure-related Territorial Assistance. The division monitors accountability issues and tracks insular area audit resolutions, including Single Audits. The Division maintains an office in Hawaii for Compact oversight in the FSM and the RMI and has a field presence in the FSM, and the RMI.

The Office of Insular Affairs is headed by the Assistant Secretary for Insular Areas, who provides overall policy direction, and a Director, who handles non-financial administrative functions, public information, and correspondence control. The Director acts on behalf of the Assistant Secretary in his absence.

Providing effective and meaningful financial assistance oversight is dependent on having the right mix of personnel skills and a carefully planned use of those skills. OIA is cognizant of the importance of human capital. Any new hiring decisions take into account expertise, diversity, and the long-term potential of new employees. All of the people OIA recruits must have the potential to work in a cross-cultural environment.

## 2014 PROGRAM PERFORMANCE

In 2014, OIA will continue to pursue the Department's mission of empowering insular communities by executing activities which improve quality of life, create economic opportunity, and promote efficient and effective governance. Improvements to quality of life and economic opportunity are achieved in a variety of ways, including funding critical infrastructure such as schools, hospitals, roads, and environmental facilities. OIA also provides assistance to help the islands identify reforms to improve their business climates. Technical assistance is provided to help the insular areas become better stewards of Federal funds, and a number of grants are now awarded according to criteria that reward good fiscal management.

With financial assistance programs exceeding $600 million per year, OIA requires sufficient personnel resources to provide oversight of grants, including Compact and mandatory Covenant CIP funding. At the 2014 level of funding OIA will:

- Improve out-year performance by grantees by continuing to focus on oversight.
- Conduct site visits to grant projects.
- Satisfy outside agencies' concern (insular governments and the GAO) of appropriate Federal involvement in grant programs.
- Continue to actively work with the U.S. Territories and the Freely Associated States to ensure their compliance with the Single Audit Act and to improve the timeliness of their audit submissions.

## Working Capital Fund

All of OIA's overhead and administrative costs that support departmental functions are paid from the Office of Insular Affairs account as assessed through the Department's Working Capital Fund as follows:

|  | 2014 |
|---|---|
| External Administrative Costs |  |
| WCF Centralized Billings | $1,022,200 |
| WCF Direct Billings/Fee for Service | $328,300 |

### Department of the Interior
### Office of Insular Affairs
### EMPLOYEE COUNT BY GRADE

*(Total Employment\*)*

| | 2012 Actual | 2013 Estimate | 2014 Estimate |
|---|---|---|---|
| SES | 1 | 1 | 1 |
| SL-0 | 1 | 1 | 1 |
| GS-15 | 5 | 5 | 5 |
| GS-14 | 8 | 9 | 9 |
| GS-13 | 13 | 14 | 16 |
| GS-12 | 6 | 5 | 4 |
| GS-11 | 1 | 1 | 2 |
| GS-10 | 0 | 0 | 0 |
| GS-9 | 0 | 2 | 0 |
| GS-8 | 0 | 0 | 0 |
| GS-7 | 0 | 1 | 1 |
| GS-6 | 1 | 0 | 0 |
| GS-5 | 0 | 1 | 1 |
| GS-4 | 1 | 1 | 1 |
| GS-3 | 0 | 0 | 0 |
| GS-2 | 0 | 0 | 0 |
| Total Employment (actual/projected) at the end of the Fiscal Year | 37 | 41 | 41 |

\*Includes two American Samoa judges (SL-1 & GS-15)and one CNMI Ombudsman (GS-14) which are funded through the American Samoa Operations and General Technical Assistance programs not OIA's operations account.

2.

| Activity: | **Territorial Assistance** | | | | | |
|---|---|---|---|---|---|---|
| Subactivity: | **General Technical Assistance** $(000) | | | | | |
| | | | **2014** | | | |
| | *2013 Full Yr. CR (PL 112-175)* | **2012 Enacted** | **Fixed Costs & Related Changes (+/-)** | **Program Changes (+/-)** | **Budget Request** | **Change from 2012 (+/-)** |
| General Technical Assistance | *13,889* | 18,774 | 0 | -1,270 | 17,504 | -1,270 |
| *Compact Impact Discretionary.* | | [4,992] | | | | |
| **TOTAL** | *13,889* | **18,774** | **0** | **-1,270** | **17,504** | **-1,270** |
| **FTEs** | *1* | **1** | **0** | **0** | **1** | **0** |

## SUMMARY OF 2014 PROGRAM CHANGES

| **Request Component** | | |
|---|---|---|
| Program Changes | Amount | FTE |
| General Technical Assistance | -1,270 | 0 |

## JUSTIFICATION OF 2014 PROGRAM CHANGES

The 2014 budget provides $17.5 million for General Technical Assistance. Discretionary Compact Impact funding of $5.0 million is moved from General Technical Assistance in 2012 to its own budget line in 2014 and funded at $3.0 million to implement a comprehensive plan to mitigate the impacts and costs of Compact migration. Without the Compact Impact funds, General Technical Assistance increases $3.7 million from the 2012 level of $13.8 million.

PROGRAM OVERVIEW

The Office of Insular Affairs' (OIA) Technical Assistance program (TAP) was authorized in Section 601 of Public Law 96-597 on December 24, 1980. The law as amended reads:
The Secretary of the Interior is authorized to extend to the governments of American Samoa, Guam, the Northern Mariana Islands, the Virgin Islands, and the Trust Territory of the Pacific Islands, and their agencies and instrumentalities, with or without reimbursement, technical assistance on subjects within the responsibility of the respective territorial governments. Such assistance may be provided by the Secretary of the Interior through members of his staff, reimbursements to other departments or agencies of the Federal Government under sections 1535 and 1536 of Title 31, grants to or cooperative agreements with such governments, agreements with Federal agencies or agencies of State or local governments, or the employment of private individuals, partnerships, or corporations. Technical assistance may include research, planning assistance, studies, and demonstration projects.

The purpose of the technical assistance program is to fund priority projects for which there are little to no funds available from other Federal agencies. The program provides the flexibility needed to respond to urgent, immediate needs in the insular areas. This flexibility is not available in any other Federal budget due to the nature of the appropriations process.

A major change that has occurred since the initial authorization of the technical assistance program is that the Administration has recognized that some programs are necessary on an ongoing basis for the insular areas; including, but not limited to: ongoing financial management, management and audit training for all insular areas. The ongoing programs were incorporated into the technical assistance program because there was no other source of funds in the Federal budget for these projects. For example, Close-Up Foundation grants, Junior Statesman grants, Pacific Basin Development Center grants, RMI 4 Atoll Healthcare Program, Prior Service Benefits program and Judicial Training are all funded through technical assistance each year.

The General Technical Assistance program provides support not otherwise available to the insular areas to meet immediate needs and to combat deteriorating economic and fiscal conditions and to maintain the momentum needed to make and sustain meaningful systemic changes. The program allows each government to identify pressing issues and priorities, and develop action plans to mitigate these problems. Direct grants and reimbursable agreements with technical assistance providers, both within and outside the Federal government, are key to implementation. Funded projects are focused to meet immediate needs in the short term and assist the governments in developing longer term solutions.

OIA staff and outside experts provide information on a variety of topics to help improve government operations in areas such as financial management, procurement and contract management, and the administration of Federal grant programs.

## 2014 PROGRAM PERFORMANCE

In 2013 and 2014, it is anticipated that approximately $5 million of the TAP funds will be utilized for grants provided directly to each insular area.    In fiscal year 2012, the four U.S. territories and the three freely associated states submitted technical assistance requests totaling approximately $50 million. OIA technical assistance funds were not sufficient to meet these requests; approximately $21 million was awarded based upon availability of funding. Please see the table on the following page.

## Technical Assistance
## Grant Awards 2012/Estimate for 2013 & 2014
### (Dollars in Thousands)

| Recipient | 2012 Awards | 2013 Estimate | 2014 Estimate |
|---|---|---|---|
| **Direct Grants to Insular Areas** | | | |
| American Samoa | 842 | TBD | TBD |
| Northern Mariana Islands (CNMI) | 2,000 | TBD | TBD |
| Guam | 3,110 | TBD | TBD |
| U.S. Virgin Islands | 4,062 | TBD | TBD |
| Federated States of Micronesia (FSM) | 504 | TBD | TBD |
| Republic of the Marshall Islands (RMI) | 516 | TBD | TBD |
| Republic of Palau | - | TBD | TBD |
| **Total, Direct Grants to Insular Areas** | **$11,034** | **$5,208** | **$5,208** |
| | | | |
| **Other TAP (Provides Benefits to Multiple Insular Areas)** | **2012 Awards** | **2013 Estimate** | **2014 Estimate** |
| Grad. School PITI VITI www.pitiviti.org -increase reflects absorption of FAS Compact area support projects | $1,876 | $2,500 | $2,500 |
| | | | |
| U.S. Bureau of Commerce, BEA (for GDP data) | $750 | $750 | $750 |
| Close Up Foundation | $1,075 | $1,075 | $1,075 |
| U.S. Department of Energy (NREL) | $434 $2,119 | $0 | $0 |
| Junior Statesman | $357 | $357 | $357 |
| Pacific Basin Development Council | $150 | TBD | TBD |
| 4 Atoll Health Care Program (RMI) | $990 | $990 | $990 |
| Prior Service Benefits Program | $1,000 | $1,000 | $1,000 |
| Judicial Training | $320 | $320 | $320 |
| CDC | $50 | $50 | $50 |
| CNMI Ombudsman's Office | $250 | $250 | $250 |
| CNMI Immigration, Labor and Law Enforce. & Forum Economic Labor Dev. (FELD) | $150 | TBD | TBD |
| *COMPACT IMPACT discretionary* | *$4,992* | *See New Line Item* | *See New Line Item* |
| **Total, Multiple Jurisdiction Programs** | **$9,521** | **$7,292** | **$7,292** |
| **Total, Technical Assistance Projects Awarded** | **$20,555** | **$12,500** | **$12,500** |

OIA requests that applicants submit Technical Assistance requests through www.grants.gov.

Review meetings are held with senior staff and the Technical Assistance Division to review and discuss submissions made by each insular area. Input is solicited from OIA field staff as well. Projects are selected for funding based on the results of these meetings and information provided by the insular area governments.

General Technical Assistance funding priorities include, but are not limited to projects which foster the development of the insular areas in the following categories: accountability; financial management; tax systems and procedures; insular management controls; economic development; training/education; energy; public safety, cultural preservation, health, immigration, labor, and law enforcement.

__Direct Grants to Insular Areas__

In 2012, $11.0 million in Technical Assistance funds were provided as direct grants to the seven insular areas. Examples of awarded grants include:

- $1,858,000 for the U.S. Virgin Islands, Juan F. Luis Hospital. Funds to address information technology deficiencies to (1) improve healthcare quality and outcomes; (2) address patient safety and federal regulatory requirements; (3) improve widespread, "meaningful use" electronic health record (EHR) adoption; and (4) reduce overall healthcare costs.
- $445,000 for the U.S. Virgin Islands. Funds to develop and implement a central cancer registry ($418K), and automate the Dept. of Health's Board licensing, credentialing and renewal processes ($27K).
- $933,000 for Guam Bureau of Revenue and Taxation. Funding for system to automate tax collection processes to address audit findings and to prevent fraud.
- $424,000 for Guam. Funding for the purchase of three (3) new ambulances.
- $312,600 for American Samoa Immunization Mobile Van to be utilized to provide health services to the community.
- $225,454 for Commonwealth of the Northern Mariana Islands Public School System Classroom Instruction That Works (CITW) Sustainability training, School Sustainability through Success In Sight: Implementation and Management of Change training, and Using Technology with Classroom Instruction that Works training.
- $269,000 for Commonwealth of the Northern Mariana Islands. Funds for aquaponics system education and training for 5 candidates from Rota to be sent to partake in Aquaponics Program for 6 months and the development of 3 stand alone aquaponics demonstration systems (demonstration facility).
- $136,160 for Commonwealth of the Northern Mariana Islands. Funding to purchase three police village patrol vehicles for Saipan.
- $110,000 for Republic of the Marshall Islands, Office of the Auditor General. Funds were provided to recruit a Certified Fraud Examiner to assist with the on-going review of alleged fraud and embezzlement of public funds in the RMI.

- $250,000 for Federated States of Micronesia, Pohnpei Port Authority. Funding provided to purchase much needed safety and security equipment, as well as repairs for current working equipment at the airport and seaport.

**Statistical Improvement Program** *(GDP Project with U.S. Department of Commerce, Bureau of Economic Analysis (BEA))*

One of OIA's goals is to improve the quality and quantity of economic data in the territories. The first place to look for economic data is GDP data and there were no official GDP data for the U.S. Territories. In December 2008, OIA completed a Memorandum of Understanding (MOU) with the Bureau of Economic Analysis (BEA) of the Department of Commerce to develop GDP data for the four U.S. Territories (American Samoa, Guam, Commonwealth of the Northern Mariana Islands, and the U.S. Virgin Islands). The initial agreement with BEA was structured for a period of 18 months for a total cost of $1.6 million. In 2012, OIA paid $750,000 to BEA to continue this project.

To calculate U.S. GDP, the BEA collects all the data it needs from other Federal agencies such as the Census Bureau, the Bureau of Labor Statistics (a DOL agency), and the IRS. Because the territories are not included in most of the current data and research work by Federal agencies, the BEA has to collect the data in the territories (hence travel) and put them in a format they use for U.S. GDP calculations. Since territorial data sources are not as extensive as those for the 50 states and DC and not as readily available, it takes more work, time and resources to put them together in the format consistent with the BEA's framework for U.S. GDP.

The first set of GDP estimates for the four territories was released on May 5, 2010, which covered the period of 2002-2007. Estimates for 2008 and 2009 were released in the spring and summer of 2011 and estimates for 2010 were released in the fall of 2012. With the 2010 estimates released in 2012, the territories are now on the same schedule as the 50 states and the District of Columbia (DC). Additional details are available at the BEA web site which can be reached through the link below:

http://www.bea.gov/national/gdp_territory.htm

This GDP measurement project represents an important first step toward achieving BEA and OIA's ultimate goal: to integrate these territories not only into the estimates of national GDP but also into the full set of the national income and product accounts (NIPAs). Currently, the NIPAs cover the 50 states and the District of Columbia, and transactions with the territories are included in transactions with the "rest-of-the world." OIA is working with the territories and the BEA to move this program forward, consulting with the territories on how to expand the program within its current structure and reach a point at which all the territories have current GDP data produced by the BEA with minimal OIA intervention.

In 2012, additional funds were provided to begin expanding the Territorial GDP Accounts to include additional information that is useful to gauge the economic performance of the island economies. BEA identified a number of new statistics that provide insight into the dynamics of the territorial economies. These new statistics are of great value to both the territorial governments and to the OIA. Examples of new statistics for which additional funding was provided in 2012 include:

- GDP by Industry Statistics—These new statistics would provide an industry-by-industry break out of economic activity and would show the share of each industry, or sector, in the economy and how much that industry, or sector, contributed to overall real GDP growth or decline. The new measures would also show how much each industry contributed to the overall inflation rate for the economy.
- Compensation of Employees by Industry—These new statistics would provide estimates of wages and salaries, as well as estimates of supplements to wages and salaries (employer contributions to social security, employer contributions to health insurance, employer contributions to unemployment insurance, etc.) for each industry, or sector, in the economy. These new measures would be particularly useful for tracking wage and salary trends for key industries, or sectors, within the territorial economies.
- Detailed Consumer Spending—These new statistics would provide additional information on the components of "Personal Consumption Expenditures" and would be available on both a nominal and a real basis. The new measures would show how household spending patterns have changed over time and how the composition of products, or commodities, purchased by households has changed.

### Republic of the Marshall Islands 4 Atoll Healthcare Program

The Four Atoll Health Care Program addresses the medical needs of Marshall Islands communities affected by the nuclear weapons testing program which the U.S. Department of Defense carried out in the Marshall Islands between 1946 and 1958. General Technical Assistance provides for the primary health care needs of the Enewetak, Bikini, Rongelap and Utrik communities in the Republic of the Marshall Islands. In 2012, the Technical Assistance program funded $990,203 for medical professionals and needed medical supplies for the population of the 4 Republic of the Marshall Islands Atolls of Kili/Bikini – 1,198 people; Enewetak/Ujelang - 612 people; Rongelap/Mejatto – 551 people; Utrik- 425 people and Ejit – 245 people.

- The funds provided a full time primary care physician to each of the four atolls to work in collaboration with a full time island based health assistant.
- Improve Access to Quality and Specialty Care Services; Reduce Inter-Island Referrals for Secondary Care; Improve Overall Health of the Communities Served; Utilize the full potential of our doctors for better delivery of service; Conduct drinking water quality test for presence of Pathogens.
- Through these goals they were able to replace one primary care Physician; begin Visual Impairment Screening by primary care physicians; Increase access to specialty clinics for Diabetes, Hypertension, Well Baby, and Reproductive Health; Improve maternal and child care programs.

The Marshall Islands Ministry of Health provides local support to this Interior-funded program.

**Prior Service Benefits Program**

In the last days of World War II, Micronesians started working for the U.S. Military providing essential services to active duty soldiers, sailors and airmen, including care for the wounded and support for the men fighting in places like Iwo Jima and Okinawa. These people were paid very low meager salaries, often as low as 9 cents an hour, with no employee benefits. The Prior Service Benefits Trust Fund provides payments to beneficiaries that are citizens of the Commonwealth of the Northern Mariana Islands, Federated States of Micronesia, the Republic of the Marshall Islands and the Republic of Palau who worked for the U.S. Department of Navy and the U.S. Trust Territory of the Pacific Islands for the period from 1944 through June 30, 1968. The Prior Service Benefits Trust Fund helps ensure the solvency of the Fund so that payments to beneficiaries will continue uninterrupted. Without the funds provided by OIA, the Prior Service Benefits Trust fund will be unable to continue payments to its beneficiaries. Checks are sent out from this fund on a monthly basis. Currently, there are no funds available for any additional payments beyond those funds provided by OIA. Funds are desperately needed in order to allow the Prior Service Benefits Trust Fund to continue to make the monthly payments.

OIA made available $1,000,000 in 2012 to support the Prior Service Trust Fund Administration (PSTFA).

**Commonwealth of the Northern Mariana Islands Immigration, Labor and Law Enforcement Program**

The CNMI Initiative on Labor, Immigration and Law Enforcement was established by Congress 1995 to address immigration, labor, and related law enforcement problems in the Commonwealth of the Northern Mariana Islands. It was subsequently funded through the Covenant through 2004. Beginning in 2005, activities in support of the CNMI Initiative have been funded under General Technical Assistance due to the fact that the 2005 House of Representatives Report #108-542 requests that OIA continue the CNMI immigration initiative and the labor ombudsman office out of technical assistance funds. The CNMI Initiative addresses immigration, labor and related law enforcement problems through a variety of means including reimbursable agreements with other Federal Agencies and grants funding labor, immigration, and law enforcement personnel within the Commonwealth's Office of the Attorney General and the Department of Labor.

In 2012, $150,000 in total was requested and provided to continue support for an Assistant U.S. Attorney (AUSA) positions in the Saipan Field Office. These AUSA positions are devoted entirely to enforcement of federal laws addressing the labor, immigration and law enforcement initiative.

In 2012, $136,000 was requested and provided to purchase 3 additional law enforcement patrol vehicles. No additional labor, immigration or law enforcement funds were requested.

Forum on Economic and Labor Development (FELD)

In order to comply with Public Law 110-229, Consolidated Natural Resources Act (CNRA), May 8, 2008, Title VII, Section 702e, Assistant Secretary of the Interior for Insular Areas convened a public meeting, *Forum on Economic and Labor Development (FELD)*, on Saipan on November 9, 2010, as a step toward fulfilling requirements of the law. The FELD attracted a representative cross section of leaders from the CNMI government, business, labor and community groups. The main purpose of the forum was to gather ideas and suggestions from all stakeholders and identify areas of the CNMI economy and labor market that would benefit the most from a technical assistance grant OIA may make available under the law. In an all-day proceedings that included general as well as breakout sessions, participants produced a detailed list of areas that, in their opinions, would benefit from federal grants and contribute to economic growth and financial stability.

The list includes all major areas of the economy and labor market that FELD participants felt would benefit from direct federal assistance. The list also includes subsidies for existing industries to reduce consumer cost of necessities such as power and transport as well as funds for building new facilities such as a Micronesian Cultural Center and a state-of-the-art hospital.

The list of ideas and suggestions for economic growth and financial stability is fairly broad and wide ranging. It covers many areas that would undoubtedly help the CNMI's economy and its financial stability if they were funded. However public law 110-229, which extended federal immigration rules and regulations to the CNMI and assigned implementation responsibility to DOI and other federal agencies, does not appropriate funds for the technical assistance grant implementation it mandates. In the absence of resources specifically committed to this purpose, OIA has to divert resources from other uses to implement CNRA's technical assistance provisions. This commitment adds to the financial constraints within which OIA has to allocate its limited Technical Assistance budget that has recently been reduced because of government-wide fiscal constraints.

OIA's resource constraints severely limit its capacity to aid the CNMI and implement the CNRA's mandate for technical assistance. Still, to fulfill requirements of the law and offer the CNMI some critically needed economic and financial aid, OIA provided a grant of $1 million from its existing General Technical Assistance funding and other scarce resources.

In 2012, no further FELD grants were awarded. The existing 2011 FELD grant remains open and still has a balance available of $681,639.

Ombudsman's Office (Saipan, CNMI)

The Federal Ombudsman's Office provides assistance to the Commonwealth of the Northern Mariana Islands' 30,000 plus nonresident workers with labor and immigration complaints. The Federal Ombudsman's Office has a staff of professional caseworker/interpreters who speak Mandarin, Taiwanese, Tagalog, Bengali, Hindu, Urdu and Singhalese. Technical Assistance funds are utilized to pay for the operations of the Ombudsman's Office. The cost for operation of the Ombudsman's Office is estimated at $250,000 annually.

**Close Up Program**

The Close Up Foundation has conducted the Close Up Insular Areas Program under a grant from the General Technical Assistance program since 1988. Close Up was provided $1.075 million in funds in 2012 and conducted civic education work with students, teachers and administrators from American Samoa, the Commonwealth of the Northern Mariana Islands, Guam, the Federated States of Micronesia, the Republic of the Marshall Islands, the Republic of Palau, and the U.S. Virgin Islands.

The goals of Close Up's Insular Areas Program for students and teachers are to: demonstrate how the United States' model of democracy functions and to foster the interest, knowledge, and skills needed to effectively participate in a democracy; address the academic needs of the insular areas and to provide training and materials to improve teachers' civic education skills; and increase mutual understanding between the United States' diverse citizenry with a special emphasis on public policy concerns and culture.

The technical assistance grant will provide funds for students and teachers from American Samoa, Commonwealth of the Northern Mariana Islands, Guam, Federated States of Micronesia, Republic of the Marshall Islands, Republic of Palau and the United States Virgin Islands to travel and participate on Close Up Washington civic education programs and for Close Up to conduct multi-day island-based student centric civic education programs.

The principal components of the Close Up Insular Areas Program were: High School Student participation in a week-long Close Up Washington High School civic education program; Participation by high school students and teachers from the Pacific Islands on additional study visits to Williamsburg, Virginia; Philadelphia, PA and New York, NY; Middle School Student participation in a Close Up Washington Middle School civic education program which may have included a Philadelphia study visit component; Teacher participation in a parallel Close Up Washington Program for Educators; High School Student participation in three-day Close Up Youth Summit civic education programs held in American Samoa, Commonwealth of the Northern Mariana Islands, Guam, and the U.S. Virgin Islands; Financial and technical support of locally organized "Close Up" civic education programs; Professional evaluation of the program to ensure that academic goals and objectives are met.

Close Up conducted Close Up Insular Areas Washington Programs in Spring 2012. In all, 232 students and 32 teachers from the Insular Areas travelled to Washington D.C. to participate in Close Up programs. High School Groups from the Pacific Islands participated in a June 7-20 Washington program with additional visits to Williamsburg, Philadelphia and New York. High School and Middle Groups from the U.S. Virgin Islands participated on Close Up Washington Programs in April and June 2012. Additionally, a Middle School group from Guam participated on a Close Up Washington Middle School program in May 2012. The students visit the historical and cultural attractions of the Nation's capital, participate in workshop and simulations with other students, attend sessions with prominent Washington leaders, and visit with their Congressional and Embassy representatives.

Insular areas students and teachers participate on Close Up Washington programs alongside their peers from around the United States. This further integrates the island participants into American education and culture and exposes students from across our nation to the strategic importance and cultural uniqueness of the island communities.

Teachers participate on the Close Up Washington Program for Educators, a unique professional development provides for sessions with education experts and collaboration with peers from around the United States. The program provides training and materials to improve teacher civic education skills in the island communities.

Close Up conducted its locally-based three-day Youth Summit civic education programs in American Samoa, Commonwealth of the Northern Mariana Islands and Guam and the U.S. Virgin Islands in October 2012. The Youth Summit programs allow students to identify and research public policy issues and community concerns, develop a consensus based "Agenda for Policy Action" with their peers, and present their ideas to local government officials.

Close Up also financially or administratively supported local programming in the Federated States of Micronesia and Palau. The Federated States of Micronesia Department of Education conducted a February 2012 program "Economic Reforms, Facing the Challenges of a Changing Economy" for 200 students. In Palau, 120 high school students participated in a program entitled "Students' Role in an Active Community" in March 2012 in Koror.

Close Up civic education programs provide young people with an understanding of the United States Government and the role that each individual plays in our democratic system. They return home inspired and possessing skills and confidence to become active participants in the civic life of their communities.

**Junior Statesman Foundation**

OIA awarded a technical assistance grant in the amount of $356,500 in 2012 for Junior Statesmen Foundation (JSF) scholarships for twenty-eight high school students from the insular areas to attend the 2012 Junior Statesmen Summer Schools. That was the 22[th] year that the Junior Statesmen Foundation has worked in partnership with the Office of Insular Affairs to identify, educate and train outstanding insular-area high school students for active, effective and ethical participation in public affairs.

Interior Department grants cover the cost of each scholarship winner's summer school tuition (including room and board on the host university campus and all related costs, as well as transportation to and from the university). The Junior Statesmen Summer School is conducted at Georgetown, Princeton and Stanford Universities.

At the month-long summer schools, students take a Political Science college level course, along with high level instruction in debate and leadership. Seven insular areas will participate in the scholarship program: American Samoa, the Northern Mariana Islands, the Federated States of Micronesia, Guam, Palau, the U.S. Virgin Islands and the Marshall Islands.

The Interior Department grant also funds academic prep programs in colleges in American Samoa, the Northern Mariana Islands, Guam, Palau and the U.S. Virgin Islands to help prepare their students for their summer school experience.

The Junior Statesmen mission is to strengthen American democracy by educating and preparing high school students for life-long involvement and responsible leadership in a democratic society.

**Pacific Basin Development Council (PBDC)**

The Governors of American Samoa, Guam, the Northern Mariana Islands and Hawaii collectively established PBDC in February 1980 to articulate and address economic and social development issues of the Pacific Islands. Its purpose is to enhance the region's economic competitiveness through its capability to identify, understand, and strategically plan. Funds are provided to the PBDC to further improve Homeland Security, Capacity building, and organizational development.

- The Governors' and Islands' staffs play an integral role in PBDC. Formal policy and project decisions are determined by the PBDC Board of Directors. The Pacific Way generally requires decisions by Board consensus, rather than majority rule.
- Each Governor appoints key aides to PBDC's Technical Advisory Committee (TAC). TAC offers alternatives (for action by the Governors); provides local coordination and follow-ups; and gives the staff guidance on day-to-day activities.
- In 2012, PBDC was granted $150,000 from OIA for continued support of the targeted areas.

**Judicial Training**

Training programs are also conducted to help the Pacific Islands face burgeoning populations and judicial systems that are not fully developed. The Pacific Islands Committee of the Ninth Circuit Judicial Council oversees, designs, arranges and ensures the delivery of these training programs and actively participates in the programs to guarantee training is provided that is responsive to educational needs. This training program was a result of an assessment that was conducted of the court systems in the American territories and the freely associated states which identified specific training needs for the non-lawyer judges, legally trained judges, and court staff in these islands. $320,000 was provided for this program in 2012 (a detailed report is available upon request).

**Technical Assistance Energy Assessment**

Energy security is critical to the insular areas' future economic development and sustainability. Development of a long-term Strategic Energy Plan is needed to achieve energy security. OIA has entered into an Inter-Agency Agreement (IAA) and provided additional funds to the U.S. Department of Energy, National Renewable Energy Laboratory (NREL) in 2012 to continue to assist the Governments of American Samoa, Commonwealth of the Northern Marianas Islands (CNMI), and Guam with developing a clean energy future for these Pacific Territories. The additional funding provided in FY 2012 now provides for inclusion of the Federated States of Micronesia, the Republic of the Marshall Islands and the Republic of Palau.

Through the IAA, NREL is providing technical support to these governments by conducting initial energy efficiency and renewable energy (EE/RE) assessments and assisting in developing a strategic plan for EE/RE implementation and deployment. NREL has sent interdisciplinary teams to cover each relevant technical area for energy assessments, system recovery, and upgrades. Experts in the following disciplines participated:

1. Integrated Wind-Diesel Generation
2. Transmission and Distribution
3. Energy Efficiency and Building Technologies
4. Solar Technologies
5. Biomass and Waste-to-Energy

Additionally, OIA, through NREL shall support the Governments with the process of developing and implementing long-term Strategic Energy Plans that will involve a range of stakeholders including government officials, private sector entities, community leaders, and appropriate federal agency partners. Support is being provided to establish Energy Steering Committees that will be charged with developing and implementing long-term Strategic Energy Plans.

Through the revised agreements, NREL shall provide technical support to the Freely Associated States of the Federated States of Micronesia, the Republic of the Marshall Islands, and the Republic of Palau, as well as the territories of Guam, American Samoa and the Northern Mariana Islands in support of OIA's initiative to assist the insular areas with their efforts to reduce energy costs and diversify away from a near total dependence on petroleum based fuels. The Scope of Work consists of the following ten overall tasks to be conducted over the course of the three years beginning in 2012.

1. Conduct literature review, with an emphasis on the 2006 Territorial Energy Assessment (http://www.doi.gov/oia/reports/iaea2006report.html) and compile background data
2. Conduct stakeholder workshop in each country (including each state of the FSM, as well as Ebeye and Majuro, RMI)
3. Assist with the formation and running of energy steering committees or energy working groups if applicable and as appropriate

4. Conduct renewable energy and energy efficiency technical assessments
5. Integrate energy data into tracking sheets and conduct wedge analysis
6. Develop an energy action plan for each country
7. Provide technical assistance to each country (including each state of the FSM, as well as Ebeye and Majuro, RMI)
8. Develop a community outreach program
9. Provide on-call technical support to OIA
10. Project management, coordination and reporting

**Programs funded by Technical Assistance and jointly managed by the Graduate School**

The mission of the U.S. Department of the Interior's Office of Insular Affairs (DOI/OIA) is to assist the U.S.-affiliated islands in "developing more efficient and effective government by providing financial and technical assistance, and help manage Federal islands relations by promoting appropriate Federal policies". As part of DOI/OIA's Technical Assistance program, the International Institute of the Graduate School USA (GS/USA) provides training and related services through the Island Training Program (ITP) to assist the insular governments to improve the financial management and program performance of the Pacific and Virgin Islands insular governments.

The Virgin Islands Training Initiative (VITI) and the Pacific Islands Training Initiative (PITI) programs were established in 1991 with the GS/USA to assist DOI/OIA in fulfilling their mission by providing training and consultative services to the U.S. Virgin Islands, American Samoa, Guam, the Commonwealth of the Northern Mariana Islands, the Republic of the Marshall Islands, the Federated States of Micronesia, and the Republic of Palau to assist the insular governments in improving their financial management and program performance . The programs are designed and delivered in a manner that complements and supports insular efforts to implement and maintain sound financial management and program performance practices.

**Strategic Planning and Implementation**

As part of its yearly planning process the Program Managers responsible for managing PITI-VITI review accomplishments, develop training plans for the next year, and budget for the planned activities. Periodically PITI-VITI management also revises its strategic plans to focus its efforts and resources on the most critical issues facing the insular governments and DOI/OIA.

In November 2011, PITI-VITI Program Managers, key DOI/OIA Technical Assistance managers and several key PITI-VITI instructors and consultants conducted a thorough review of the PITI-VITI program, its vision and mission statement, and it's strategic goals. To guide them, the review team utilized the Department of Interior's *"Strategic Plan for Fiscal years 2011-2016"* and DOI/OIA's *"Budget Justification and Performance Information for Fiscal Year 2012."* Using these documents as the drivers for PITI-VITI activities, the team then reviewed and revised the PITI-VITI's program's vision statement, mission statement, and strategic goals to better align them with DOI/OIA's goals and measures.

PITI-VITI's vision is to "provide the services that enable insular governments to use resources efficiently and effectively to promote economic growth, achieve fiscal stability, and fulfill citizens' needs."

PITI-VITI's mission is to "provide customized, results-oriented professional and organizational development services that enable insular governments to strengthen financial and program performance and accountability, achieve fiscal stability, and promote economic growth. PITI-VITI works to build trust in insular governments by fostering responsible leadership and financial stewardship of the highest standard."

Based on these vision and mission statements, PITI-VITI works to achieve the following five strategic goals:

1. Improve leadership and management capacity to effectively perform;
2. Improve financial management systems and practices;
3. Increase effectiveness and program results;
4. Institutionalize regional professional organizations and communities of practice;
5. Improve the capacity and capabilities of the public sector work force in critical positions and functions.

For each of these strategic goals PITI-VITI has developed sets of activities and performance measures. These activities, when completed, will lead to the accomplishment of the strategic goals. The performance measures are the means by which PITI-VITI can assess progress towards the goals and through which PITI-VITI can be held accountable by its stakeholders.

## II.  MAJOR REGIONAL PROGRAM INITIATIVES
### A.  Audit Improvement Project
>*Strategic Goal 1:      Improve Leadership and Management Capacity to Perform Effectively*
>*Strategic Goal 2:     Improve Financial Management Systems and Practices*

Audit improvement has become a cornerstone of the financial management improvement efforts launched more than a decade ago by DOI-OIA and PITI-VITI. PITI-VITI continues to provide technical support to improve the timeliness and effectiveness of the insular areas' single audits, building on prior successes. Between FY2003 and FY2010, financial audit qualifications within the insular areas dropped from 159 to 16, with an even lower number of audit qualifications expected with the FY2011 single audits. Between FY2007 - 2009, ten of the eleven insular governments submitted their audited financial statements on time. By FY2009 seven governments – the Republic of Palau, Pohnpei State, Kosrae State, Yap State, FSM National Government, Guam, and the Republic of the Marshall Islands received unqualified financial audit opinions, some for the first time in their history. All of the governments are working on clearing their audit findings with significant attention on the accounting cycle areas of reconciliation, cash management and fixed assets. These areas are also being tracked with interim performance measures which indicate improvement, or lack of improvement, well before the audit is issued. While the U. S. Virgin Islands has laid out a clear plan to bring their audit timely, 3 of the other insular government's single audits were significantly late in FY10 & FY11; the Republic of Palau, the Republic of the Marshall Islands, and the Commonwealth of the Northern Mariana Islands. The reasons are varied (loss of personnel, change in administration, unresolved legal issues) but PITI-VITI is working with those governments to encourage and assist the finance office where possible to bring the audit back into a timely status.

## B. Executive Leadership Development Program

> *Strategic Goal 1:    To improve leadership and management capacity to effectively perform.*
> *Strategic Goal 5:    Improve the capacity and capabilities of the public sector work force in critical positions and functions.*

All of the insular governments have a difficult time attracting and retaining qualified individuals to work in core functions of island governments. Many young, educated and promising employees are trained by local governments and are then offered higher paying jobs by component units or within the private sector. The Executive Leadership Development Program (ELDP) was designed to assist the insular governments with developing and retaining qualified and skilled staff that will become the future leaders of their respective governments. Program participants meet four times over the course of a year to develop skills in leadership, management, government finance, and project management. Twenty-One (21) participants from throughout the insular areas completed the first year of the program in September 2009. An additional twenty-five (25) participants completed the second year of the program in May 2011.

Twenty-five (25) participants from the Pacific region and the US Virgin Islands were selected as participants for the 2012-2013 ELDP class which began in July 2012. Participants will complete the first two phases of the program during 2012 and the final two stages of the program during 2013.

## C. Island Government Finance Officers Association (IGFOA)

> *Strategic Goal 3:    Increase effectiveness and program results*
> *Strategic Goal 4:    Institutionalize regional professional organizations and communities of practice.*

Since 2000, PITI-VITI has supported the efforts of the Island Government Finance Officers' Association (IGFOA), a professional organization comprised of the Chief Financial Officers of each insular government and key financial managers within each government. In addition to arranging for IGFOA members to participate in the annual Government Finance Officers Association (GFOA) Conference, PITI-VITI works with IGFOA to highlight best practices in the insular governments and to serve as a conduit for resource sharing. IGFOA gatherings enable the insular government finance community to discuss common challenges they face and identify successful best practices and strategies to address problems. PITI-VITI also takes advantage of IGFOA meetings to deliver professional development seminars on leadership skills and team building in the finance environment.

Two IGFOA conferences were held during 2012. The first 2012 IGFOA conference was held during the week of June 10 - 15 in Chicago, Illinois in conjunction with the 2012 Government Finance Officers' Association (GFOA) annual conference. The theme for both conferences was "Winds of Change: Public Finance in Transition." One component of "Winds of Change'" is GASB-54 (Fund Balance and Governmental Fund Type Reporting) and its application in government finance. Another component of the "Winds of Change" is to ensure that the operations of the government are efficiently utilizing scarce resources. This IGFOA meeting focused on implementing GASB-54 and performance measures in the finance office operations.

The second IGFOA conference was held December 4 - 6, 2012 in Lihue, Kauai, Hawaii. The Kauai IGFOA Conference concentrated on the need for the adherence to budget projections, communicating financial information to elected officials, obtaining information on recently issued GASB accounting standards, and developing cash management plans. Participants also provided updates on their government's performance measurement action plans for finance office operations and provided best practices for performance improvement and single audit coordination.

D. **Association of Pacific Islands Public Auditors (APIPA)**
  ➤*Strategic Goal 3:*    *Increase effectiveness and program results*
  ➤*Strategic Goal 4:*    *Institutionalize regional professional organizations and communities of practice.*

The Association of Pacific Islands Public Auditors (APIPA) is an association made up of public auditors from each of the insular areas. APIPA holds annual conferences to discuss issues related to the field of auditing and to provide practitioners an opportunity to attain continuing professional education training opportunities required by the field. Since its inception in 1991, PITI has provided auditors with the opportunity to attain up to 40 hours of continuing professional education (CPE) credits annually. By providing training during the annual APIPA conference and providing targeted audit training at each insular jurisdiction, PITI-VITI plays a critical role in working with APIPA to strengthen institutional support to the various public audit offices in the region.

PITI provided six (6) Graduate School USA auditing and financial management specialists/instructors who combined to deliver eighteen (18) courses for the 290 participants that attended the 23rd annual APIPA conference held in Koror, Republic of Palau, during the week of August 20-24, 2012. A total of 1,563 course certificates were awarded to conference participants. In addition, PITI-VITI also provided forty (40) hours of customized CPE training to each of the public audit offices in the U.S.-affiliated Pacific region and the U.S. Virgin Islands during 2012.

E. **Development of Insular Government** *Performeters and AFTER Analysis*
  ➤*Strategic Goal 1:*    *To improve leadership and management capacity to effectively perform.*
  ➤*Strategic Goal 3:*    *Increase effectiveness and program results*

The *Performeter* provides an independent assessment of each insular government's financial health and success, based on their audited financial statements. Using various financial ratios, most governments now have ten years of *Performeter* data with which to measure financial trends—both positive and negative. New *Performeters* were developed for seven (7) entities in 2012 based on information in each of their respective government's 2011 audited financial statements (the USVI, the Republic of Palau, the Republic of the Marshall Islands, and the CNMI are one year behind in their single audit requirements so their most recent *Performeter* were for FY 2010). Many of the insular governments use the *Perfometer* results to explain their financial status to their Legislatures and Governors, ultimately leading to better-informed fiscal decisions. The accompanying AFTER analysis included at the end of each *Performeter* details the government's efforts to develop timely and accurate financial statements.

## F. Training and Technical Assistance Support
> *Strategic Goal 1:*    *Improve Leadership and Management Capacity to Perform Effectively*
> *Strategic Goal 2:*    *Improve Financial Management Systems and Practices*
> *Strategic Goal 3:*    *Increase effectiveness and program results*
> *Strategic Goal 5:*    *Improve the capacity and capabilities of the public sector work force in critical positions and functions.*

Thirty-five (35) classroom training courses were delivered in 2012 for 2,107 course participants. These totals include seventeen classroom courses that were delivered on site for 544 participants and eighteen courses that were delivered during the 2012 APIPA conference on Palau for 1,563 course participants. Classroom training courses were delivered in Procurement and Contract Management, Human Resource Management, Supervision and Management, Governmental Accounting, Auditing, Ethics, Leadership, Fraud, Grants Management, Indirect Costs, Management and Internal Controls, and Strategic Planning. In addition, seventeen (17) consult-training activities were provided that 585 insular government employees took part in support of various government-specific initiatives.

## G. FSM and RMI Compact Support
> *Strategic Goal 1:*    *Improve leadership and management capacity to effectively perform*
> *Strategic Goal 3:*    *Increase effectiveness and program results*

PITI-VITI provides technical support to both the FSM and RMI on issues relating to Compact implementation. PITI-VITI assists both countries with preparation for technical meetings, preparation for annual JEMCO & JEMFAC meetings, and budgetary, fiscal, and sector support. Compact-specific activities have included:

- Development of Long-Term Fiscal Frameworks to plan for the remaining ten years of Compact assistance in each of the five FSM governments;
- Continued Fiscal Reform in Chuuk & Kosrae;
- Leadership, presidential and cabinet briefings on economic developments and fiscal and economic policy;
- Education reform in Chuuk, including facilitation of leadership conference to address outstanding issues;

- Mediation of Compact Infrastructure issues, including facilitation of a bilateral meeting between the FSM and US in June, 2011;
- Development and maintenance of a Compact Tracking Tool, which tracks Compact expenditures by distribution formula across FSM states;
- Review of the role and effectiveness of the Chuuk Financial Control Commission (CFCC);
- Support to the project-based proposal processes for environment, private sector and capacity building grant sectors, including template development and on-site, state-specific support in advance of US budget consultations;
- Implementation of the new Compact sector for "Enhanced Reporting and Accountability," which funds some core reporting functions of government;
- Trust Fund analysis and projections for both the FSM and RMI;
- Long-term debt analysis for the RMI, including recommendations for debt remediation

**H. Statistical and Economic Reporting for the three Freely Associated States of the Federated States of Micronesia, the Republic of the Marshall Islands, and the Republic of Palau**
> *Strategic Goal 1:*    *Improve leadership and management capacity to effectively perform*
> *Strategic Goal 3:*    *Increase        effectiveness       and       program       results*

The three Freely Associated States (FAS) of the Republic of the Marshall Islands (RMI), the Federated States of Micronesia (FSM) and the Republic of Palau (ROP) each have extensive needs for professional expertise to augment existing capacities to complete periodic reviews of their economies, and to maintain and strengthen economic statistical series to support economic monitoring and analysis. Since the economic reporting and statistical development and maintenance programs required across all three Freely Associated States are relatively similar, the Graduate School has based one highly qualified professional in the Republic of Palau to provide approximately eight (8) months per year to (a) lead the external inputs to the program in all three FAS, (b) provide direct external inputs to all three FAS to develop and/or maintain economic reporting and statistical development programs, and (c) provide extra support to Palau, given the current relatively weakened status of its economic reporting and statistics systems.

The Graduate School has assisted the FSM, RMI, and ROP with the maintenance of annual government finance statistics, the development and analysis of key economic indicators (growth, income, employment, outmigration, external debt), and an analysis of fiscal policy. These updates are captured in annual reports that help fulfill Compact mandates and, in the cases of the FSM and RMI, help JEMCO and JEMFAC direct Compact implementation. High-level briefings have been consistently delivered for US, FSM and RMI JEMCO and JEMFAC members to provide background analysis prior to annual meetings. This activity has been expanded to include Palau as of 2012, fielding a long-term regional advisor in Palau to provide regular support to the three governments for eight months of the calendar year. Outputs include:

- Annual FSM Economic Review and Statistical Appendix
- Annual RMI Economic Review and Statistical Appendix
- Annual ROP Economic Review and Statistical Appendix

I.   Financial Management Improvement Program (FMIP)
  ➤*Strategic Goal 1:*   *Improve leadership and management capacity to effectively perform*
  ➤*Strategic Goal 2:*   *Improve financial management systems and practices.*

Since 1998, PITI-VITI has worked with the insular governments to develop Financial Management Improvement Plans (FMIPs). The planning process has used the same basic formats, and a methodology that focuses on: 1) improving business processes, practices, and procedures; 2) improving innovation and utilization of information technology; and 3) developing and enhancing human resource development. In developing the FMIP plans, interdisciplinary teams are established. These teams include both a core team of government technical experts and PITI-VITI consultants who are responsible for the intensive field work required of the plan for improving innovation and utilization of information technology and a strategic planning team of senior government officials who provides leadership and direction to the core team. PITI-VITI did not conduct a FMIP during 2012.

J.  Finance and Audit Office Assessments
  ➤*Strategic Goal 1:*   *Improve leadership and management capacity to effectively perform*
  ➤*Strategic Goal 2:*   *Improve financial management systems and practices.*
  ➤*Strategic Goal 3:*   *Increase effectiveness and program results*

PITI-VITI has developed diagnostic tools to measure each insular government's audit and finance offices against a standard, broad set of criteria. PITI-VITI did not conduct any Finance or Audit Office Assessments during 2012.

3.

| Activity: Territorial Assistance | | | | | | |
|---|---|---|---|---|---|---|
| Subactivity: Maintenance Assistance $(000) | | | | | | |
| | | | **2014** | | | |
| | *2013 Full Yr. CR (PL 112-175)* | **2012 Enacted** | **Fixed Costs & Related Changes (+/-)** | **Program Changes (+/-)** | **Budget Request** | **Change from 2012 (+/-)** |
| | *2,251* | 2,237 | 0 | -1,156 | 1,081 | -1,156 |
| FTEs | *0* | 0 | 0 | 0 | 0 | 0 |

## SUMMARY OF 2014 PROGRAM CHANGES

| Request Component | | |
|---|---|---|
| Program Changes | Amount | FTE |
| Maintenance Assistance | -1,156 | 0 |

## JUSTIFICATION OF 2014 PROGRAM CHANGES

The 2014 budget request for Maintenance Assistance is $1.1 million, a general program decrease of $1.2 million from the 2012 level.

## PROGRAM OVERVIEW

The Department of the Interior will continue to provide assistance for investments in public infrastructure in the insular areas, but at a reduced level. The Maintenance Assistance fund is used to support, develop, improve, and as much possible, institutionalize infrastructure maintenance practices in the seven insular areas.

History demonstrated that the governments had placed little emphasis on maintenance planning and budgeting, life cycle costing, and training. Maintenance was a reaction to crisis, rather than a regular, institutionalized process. As a consequence, the usefulness of power plants, roads, ports, water and sewer systems, and public buildings declined prematurely. The maintenance assistance program addresses this problem by providing expert reviews and recommendations on the general condition of the infrastructure and by providing cost-shared grants to provide long-term solutions to systemic problems.

The maintenance assistance program focuses on changing those conditions that allow poor maintenance practices to exist. The program underwrites training, education, and technical advice related to maintenance. Funding can be used to purchase specialized maintenance equipment or information technology related to maintenance. The program also funds the cost of inventories of maintenance needs and the development of maintenance plans. The program provides an ongoing assessment of its effectiveness through annual site visits.

The maintenance assistance fund can also provide funding to address general regional training needs and allows the insular governments to share expertise and develop maintenance practices appropriate to the region. The Pacific Lineman Training Program makes power maintenance training easily accessible to all insular areas. The maintenance assistance program has proven to be an effective method of institutionalizing better maintenance practices throughout the U.S. affiliated islands.

Each discretionary project is analyzed on its merits, including the extent to which the project helps achieve long-term and intermediate goals and strategies. In addition, as a pre-requisite for receiving discretionary technical assistance, OIA has developed a set of threshold criteria that must be met. These criteria have been documented in a financial assistance manual.

Maintenance assistance generally uses grants as the primary means to provide insular assistance. However, grants to individual island areas usually require an equal local financial match. This strategy emphasizes the importance of local buy-in to maintenance assistance as a means of building and sustaining local institutions. Regional programs have also been developed for training purposes to emphasize economies of scale.

## 2014 PROGRAM PERFORMANCE

In 2012, the Maintenance Assistance program awarded a number of grants for programs to enhance maintenance efforts within each insular area.

An example of a direct grant to an insular area was $739,453 awarded to American Samoa in 2012 for the Comprehensive School Bus Safety Program. This program is designed to provide training to enable American Samoa Department of Education bus mechanics to maintain the school bus fleet. Furthermore, a $394,000 grant was awarded to the U.S. Virgin Islands Water and Power Authority for water line maintenance equipment. This equipment will assist in lowering the maintenance cost as well as reduce the down time of water lines while they are being repaired.

Maintenance Assistance grants support regional maintenance initiatives. One example of such an initiative is the Pacific Lineman Training Program (PLT) which hones the skills of Pacific island power employees. OIA awarded $275,000 for the PLT program in 2012 to provide 38 weeks of professional linemen training. Training includes the Basic Lineman Training Course as well as advanced training courses in Hot Line Work, and U.S. Department of Labor Certification Training. The PLT program plans to train additional linemen in 2013 and 2014. In 2013 and 2014, the Maintenance Assistance program plans to continue funding immediate needs for maintenance in the insular areas while maintaining support for regional initiatives.

The following table identifies the allocation of Maintenance Assistance funding for 2012:

**Maintenance Assistance**

**Grant Awards 2012**
**(Dollars in Thousands)**

| Recipient | 2012 Awards |
|---|---|
| **Insular Area** | |
| American Samoa | 739,453 |
| Northern Mariana Islands (CNMI) | 382,493 |
| Guam | - |
| U.S. Virgin Islands | 696,357 |
| Federated States of Micronesia (FSM) | 350,000 |
| Republic of the Marshall Islands (RMI) | - |
| Republic of Palau | 470,150 |
| Other Grants* (Regional Programs) | 374,143 |
| | |
| **Appropriated Amount** | **2,237,000** |
| **Funds available due to closeout of projects** | 775,596 |
| | |
| TOTAL | $3,012,596 |

* Includes Regional Programs which benefit the islands such as Lineman Training, Pacific Islands Power Utility Engineers Capacity Building in Demand Side Management and Training Needs Assessment of the Pacific Island power utilities and partial funding for the Board Members Workshop & Engineers Workshop.

4.

| Activity: | Territorial Assistance | | | | | |
|---|---|---|---|---|---|---|
| Subactivity: | Brown Treesnake Control | $(000) | | | | |
| | | | **2014** | | | |
| | *2013 Full Yr. CR (PL 112-175)* | **2012 Enacted** | Fixed Costs & Related Changes (+/-) | Program Changes (+/-) | **Budget Request** | Change from 2012 (+/-) |
| | *3,013* | 2,995 | 0 | +505 | 3,500 | +505 |
| FTEs | *0* | 0 | 0 | 0 | 0 | 0 |

SUMMARY OF 2014 PROGRAM CHANGES

| Request Component | | |
|---|---|---|
| Program Changes | Amount | FTE |
| Brown Treesnake Control | +505 | 0 |

JUSTIFICATION OF 2014 PROGRAM CHANGES

The 2014 budget request for Brown Treesnake Control is $3.5 million, a program increase of $505,000 with no additional FTE from the 2012 level. An additional $500,000 is being funded through the USGS to develop novel methods for detection and control of juvenile snakes, which are not susceptible to the attractant used to deliver toxicants.

PROGRAM OVERVIEW

The invasive Brown Treesnake (BTS) is believed to have been unintentionally introduced to the island of Guam following World War II. Due to an abundant prey base and an absence of natural predators, the BTS' population on Guam grew, quickly reaching unprecedented numbers. It was not until the 1980s when researchers began to study the sudden and sharp decline in Guam's bird populations that the environmental and socioeconomic damage caused by the BTS began to be understood.

The BTS is directly responsible for the extinction or local extirpation of 9 of 13 native forest birds and 3 of 12 native lizards on Guam. In addition, the BTS has had significant, negative impacts on Guam's economy. The risk of accidental transport and establishment of the BTS in other locations has impacted regional shipping and transportation through increased biosecurity needs.

The BTS caused more than 1,600 power outages in the 19-year period between 1978 and 1997. Between March 2003 and March 2004 the Guam Power Authority recorded over 195 snake-caused power outages (1 outage per 1.8 days). A single island-wide outage was estimated to cost over $3 million in lost productivity, not including repair costs, damage to electrical equipment and lost revenues. Estimates place annual costs of snake-caused outages on Guam at around $4.5 million, not including personal equipment failures, shorter equipment life span, or increased costs due to purchasing personal power generators.

An average of 170 patients per year reported snakebites to medical facilities on Guam between 1998 and 2004. A 24-month study, between 1989 and 1991, reported that 60 percent of snakebite victims treated at medical facilities on Guam were less than 6 years old.

Since Guam is a major transportation hub in the Pacific, numerous opportunities exist for this invasive species to be inadvertently introduced to other areas in the Pacific. The BTS has already been accidentally transported from Guam to other sites worldwide through infested civilian and military vessels and cargo. Documented sites include: Hawaii, the CNMI, Corpus Christi, Texas; McAlester, Oklahoma; Japan; Anchorage, Alaska; Wake Island; Taiwan; Kwajalein; Diego Garcia; Darwin, Australia; and Rota, Spain. There is appropriate concern that the introduction of the BTS to other vulnerable sites, such as Hawaii, will have similarly catastrophic ecological and economic impacts as on Guam. The potential cost of a BTS introduction on Hawaii alone has been estimated between $593 million to $2.14 billion annually.

Brown Treesnake Control is a combination research and operational program designed to prevent the dispersal of BTS from Guam to other vulnerable geographic areas and to ultimately eradicate existing or newly established BTS populations in U.S. areas. Research is conducted to improve existing BTS control tools, such as barriers, traps and baits as well as to develop better control techniques such as toxins, repellents and attractants. Research is also intended to improve our understanding of the basic biology of the BTS and to develop methods enabling large-scale suppression of BTS. It is largely accepted that severe population suppression must be achieved before eradication can be pursued. The operational program utilizes the control tools and techniques developed via the research effort to reduce the risk of BTS dispersal to other Pacific islands, the U.S. mainland, and other vulnerable locations.

The BTS Program is a cooperative effort involving primarily the Office of Insular Affairs (financial assistance and grants management); the U.S. Fish and Wildlife Service (overall program coordination); the U.S. Geological Survey (basic and applied research); the U.S. Department of Agriculture's Animal and Plant Health Inspection Service, Wildlife Services (control, management and applied research); the U.S. Department of Defense (financial assistance, control and management on military facilities); and the

Governments of Hawaii, Guam, and the Commonwealth of the Northern Mariana Islands (restoration of native species on Guam, control, management and prevention).

**2014 PROGRAM PERFORMANCE**

Although OIA has not received 2014 BTS funding proposals or awarded all of its 2013 BTS funding, it is anticipated that the funds will be used in a manner similar to 2012, as detailed below:

- The U.S. Department of Agriculture's Animal and Plant Health Inspection Service, Wildlife Services (WS), will continue its Guam-based operational BTS control program on and around commercial facilities operated by the Government of Guam and private entities. Current operations will be maintained at A.B. Won Pat International Airport, Commercial Port of Guam and commercial transportation and cargo facilities, aimed at reducing the risk of BTS dispersal to other Pacific islands, the U.S. mainland, and other locations at risk. WS will incorporate an integrated wildlife damage management approach to BTS containment using the following types of activities: detector dogs, traps, nighttime fence searches, oral toxicants, barriers, prey reduction, and public outreach activities. WS staff will ensure inspection of at least 90 percent of commercial cargo and aircraft departing Guam.

- The CNMI Department of Lands and Natural Resources, Division of Fish and Wildlife (DFW), will continue to operate a BTS interdiction program on the islands of Saipan, Tinian and Rota and ensure that, at the minimum, a 90 percent canine inspection rate of Guam-based cargo arrivals is reached and subsequently maintained. DFW will also maintain BTS traps at CNMI ports of entry and conduct public outreach.

- The Hawaii Department of Agriculture, Plant Quarantine Branch, will continue its BTS interdiction program (currently consisting of visual searches of flights and cargo by trained inspection staff) while working to reinstate its BTS Detector Dog Program which was eliminated in June 2009 due to the State's economic downturn. The Plant Quarantine Branch also plans to increase its rapid response capacity, readiness and capabilities for snake sightings in Hawaii.

- The Guam Department of Agriculture, Division of Aquatic and Wildlife Resources (DAWR), will continue its native species restoration efforts, including the Cocos Island restoration project, which has resulted in the release and establishment of Guam Rails (a BTS extirpated native bird species) on Cocos Island, a 33.6 hectare, BTS-free, atoll off the southern coast of Guam. DAWR will also continue its BTS public outreach and awareness campaigns intended to garner support and cooperation for the Cocos Island biosecurity measures intended to protect the newly established Guam Rail population.

- The U.S. Department of Agriculture's Animal and Plant Health Inspection Service, Wildlife Services, National Wildlife Research Center (NWRC) will continue conducting research designed to improve existing BTS control techniques as well as develop new ones. NWRC will continue the development of an aerial bait suppression system intended to reduce BTS populations on a landscape scale.

- USGS researchers will continue the development and testing of tools intended to improve BTS interdiction, control, and management. Research will focus on developing better methods for the control and capture of juvenile snakes, as well as landscape-level snake control. The USGS Rapid Response Team will continue to respond to snake sightings and will conduct site response training to snake searchers in the Pacific region.

- USFWS will continue to provide overall BTS program coordination on a regional and national level to ensure continued forward progress. USFWS will also continue to provide technical assistance to program partners and develop a strategic planning document for the program.

5.

| Activity: | **Territorial Assistance** | | | | | |
| Subactivity: | **Coral Reef Initiative (CRI)  $(000)** | | | | | |

| | | | 2014 | | | |
| | | | Fixed Costs & Related Changes (+/-) | Program Changes (+/-) | Budget Request | Change from 2012 (+/-) |
| | *2013 Full Yr. CR (PL 112-175)* | **2012 Enacted** | | | | |
| | 1,004 | 998 | 0 | +2 | 1,000 | +2 |
| FTEs | 0 | 0 | 0 | 0 | 0 | 0 |

## SUMMARY OF 2014 PROGRAM CHANGES

| **Request Component** | | |
| --- | --- | --- |
| Program Changes | Amount | FTE |
| Coral Reef Initiative | +2 | 0 |

## JUSTIFICATION OF 2014 PROGRAM CHANGES

The 2014 budget request for the Coral Reef Initiative is $1.0 million, a program increase of $2,000 with no change in FTE from the 2012 level.  An additional $500,000 is being funded through the USGS to conduct additional research on coral reef in the insular areas.

## PROGRAM OVERVIEW

Healthy coral reef resources are an integral part of the economy and environment of island communities, from the U.S. Virgin Islands to Guam. Among the most diverse and biologically complex ecosystems on earth, coral reefs protect island communities from coastal erosion and storm damage, provide habitat to numerous species, and support important tourism and recreational industries.  Coral reef resources are now threatened by a variety of stresses including poor water quality, over-harvesting of coral, coastal development, disease and bleaching (loss of symbiotic algae).  According to recent estimates, more than 25 percent of the world's coral reefs already have been lost or severely damaged.

Executive Order 13089 (June 1998) established the U.S. Coral Reef Task Force (Task Force) to bring together Federal, State, and territorial governments to address the coral reef crisis.  In 2001, the freely associated states (FAS) became non-voting members of the Task Force. Co-chaired by the Secretaries of the Interior and Commerce, the Task Force is credited with setting the national and international agenda for long-term management and protection of coral reefs. The insular governors, FAS presidents and the All Islands Coral Reef Committee provide significant guidance and direction to the Task Force.

With the majority of U.S. coral reefs located in the insular areas, the Office of Insular Affairs (OIA) plays a critical role in the national effort to develop effective programs to sustainably manage and protect U.S. coral reef resources. OIA has worked closely with the islands to identify and implement a broad scope of management actions from education and outreach to watershed restoration and the establishment of marine protected areas. Each island has established its own local advisory committee for strategic planning and priority setting. OIA has also supported the development and implementation of pioneering resource management efforts in the FAS, including the development of a blueprint for creating a national system of protected areas for the FSM, support for the Micronesia Challenge, natural resource assessments of the atolls of the Marshall Islands, and protection of critical marine resources in the Republic of Palau.

OIA will continue to work with the insular areas to identify, prioritize and fund local initiatives aimed at improving coral reef management, protection, and restoration in the insular areas. Priority projects are outlined in the "All Islands Coral Reef Initiative Strategy", the insular areas' "Local Action Strategies (LAS)", biodiversity and management plans developed by the FAS and the Task Force's "National Action Plan to Conserve Coral Reefs", a comprehensive program of research, mapping, monitoring, conservation and management. LAS are updated regularly by each of the insular areas and form the basis for a significant portion of the annual grant awards. Members of the Coral Reef Task Force meet semi-annually to evaluate progress and work out specific plans and priorities for the next half-year. OIA is also actively engaged in advancing efforts to establish a new research and education in St. Croix, USVI that will provide not only world-class science and educational opportunities for the Virgin Islands and across the region, but serve as a model for green building design and operations to island communities.

## 2014 PROGRAM PERFORMANCE

The goal of the Coral Reef Initiative program is to improve the health of coral reefs in the U.S. insular areas for their long-term economic and social benefit through enhanced local management and protection. OIA's primary role is to assist the insular areas in identifying causes for coral reef decline, assessing needs for improving local management and protection, and as available, providing technical and financial assistance to meet priority needs. Performance indicators and outputs will focus on the health and management of local coral reefs through assistance provided.

OIA has worked with local coral reef advisory groups to update their Local Action Strategies. These LAS identify short and long-term priority needs to improve the health and protection of their coral reefs. OIA is funding these priority needs in accordance with specific goals and objectives, with measures identified within the grants. The priorities identified in the LAS will help the insular areas reduce land-based sources of pollution, reduce over-fishing, and improve local understanding of the value of coral reefs through outreach and education programs.

Through financial and technical assistance, OIA has supported the development of several new initiatives. Among these is the Micronesia Challenge, launched at the Task Force meeting in Palau in 2005 by the region's heads of governments. The Micronesia Challenge is a bold initiative to conserve 30 percent of near-shore marine resources and 20 percent of forest resources by 2020. The challenge far exceeds current goals of international conventions and emphasizes the need for Micronesian leaders to work together to confront environmental and sustainable development issues.

Funds provided by OIA, have helped Guam and the CNMI develop significant plans to restore three watersheds, two on Guam and one on Saipan that will alleviate the effects of run-off and other threats to the adjacent coral reefs. OIA has also supported development and management of marine protected areas in the insular areas, education and internship opportunities for students in the insular areas, conservation planning for local governments, development of fisheries management plans, assessments and management of the effects of climate change on reef ecosystems, and development of resource management plans for communities in the Marshall Islands.

OIA, in cooperation with other Federal, local and international partners, supported the development of "A Blueprint for Conserving the Biodiversity of the Federated States of Micronesia". The Blueprint provides a framework for creating the first national system of protected areas for the FSM and serves as a model for the region. OIA is now supporting implementation of many of the Blueprint's goals, including the Conservation Action Planning (CAP) process to guide local site conservation actions, establishing partnerships to support and implement conservation interventions, and conducting marine resources assessments in areas with data gaps such as Kosrae and Pohnpei. OIA's support for the Blueprint's goals and objectives has also led to the creation of the Pacific Islands Managed and Protected Area Communities (PIMPAC). PIMPAC is working across the region to advance local community support for marine protection and management.

Specific ongoing outputs for the Coral Reef program include:

- Partnering with the National Park Service (NPS) and a consortium of universities known as the Joint Institute for Caribbean Marine Studies (JICMS) to establish a new marine research and education center in St. Croix, USVI. The Salt River Bay Marine Research and Education Center (MREC) will be a nexus for marine research and education in the Caribbean, supporting science-based decision making for managers throughout the region, providing education and outreach to students and the public, and restoring a world-class facility to the island. The MREC will incorporate some of the most advanced concepts for sustainable building design, making it a model for island communities. OIA is meeting regularly with the partners to complete the design phase and build institutional capacity to address the NPS's requirements for a project of this scope and complexity. OIA supported an international student design competition for the MREC in

2011/2012 that not only produced innovative green building designs but helped to raise awareness of the project around the world.

- Support for the first JICMS-led scientific study at the MREC site. The multi-disciplinary team is investigating the rare phenomenon of bioluminescence in Mangrove Lagoon and developing recommendations on ways to sustain it.
- Support for Conservation Action Planning (CAP) to guide site conservation actions in Micronesia. The CAP process helps local jurisdictions identify long-term measurable conservation results at the local level; establish partnerships to support and implement conservation actions; and quantitatively and qualitatively measure conservation effects over time. CAP is being used by some jurisdictions to update their Local Action Strategies.
- Support for community-based marine conservation planning and management in communities of the Marshall Islands, including Majuro, Arno, Ailinginae, Rongelap, Namdrik, Mili and Ailuk Atolls. These efforts will further the goal of assisting communities with resource management planning in all of the 21 inhabited atolls by 2014.
- Support for development of watershed management plans for Guam, Saipan and American Samoa that will mitigate impacts to adjacent reefs from erosion, sedimentation and storm water run-off.
- Support for community-based monitoring and management of the marine resources of Ulithi Atoll, Yap, FSM.
- Support for environmental education including eco-camps and e-learning programs in the Northern Mariana Islands and Guam.
- Support for assessing the effects of climate change on local reefs to reduce stresses and improve reef resilience.
- Support for development of community-based marine protected areas in American Samoa, Guam and CNMI, including marine resource assessments, community outreach and education and marine enforcement.
- Assistance to Guam to identify and mitigate potential threats to their coral reefs from the proposed military build-up.
- Support to advance the goals of the Micronesia Challenge including training for community-led enforcement and compliance activities and development of regional ecological indicators.
- Support for the Caribbean Challenge Initiative to work cooperatively in the region to protect and sustainably manage marine and coastal resources.
- Support for the development of the Coastal Studies Outpost (CSO) at Salt Bay National Historic Park and Ecological Preserve. The CSO will facilitate marine education and research and promote the protection of St. Croix's fisheries, shorelines and reefs.
- Support for the Governor Tauese Sunia Memorial Summer Internships that sponsor university students from the insular areas to work on the U.S. Coral Reef Task Force's Watershed Partnership Initiative projects in Hawaii, Puerto Rico and American Samoa. Actions will help reduce land-based pollution and improve coral reef health in adjacent waters.

6.

| Activity: | Territorial Assistance | | | | | |
| Subactivity: | Water & Wastewater   $(000) | | | | | |

| | 2013 Full Yr. CR (PL 112-175) | 2012 Enacted | 2014 | | | Change from 2012 (+/-) |
| | | | Fixed Costs & Related Changes (+/-) | Program Changes (+/-) | Budget Request | |
| | 795 | 790 | 0 | -790 | 0 | -790 |
| FTEs | 0 | 0 | 0 | 0 | 0 | 0 |

SUMMARY OF 2014 PROGRAM CHANGES

| Request Component | | |
| --- | --- | --- |
| Program Changes | Amount | FTE |
| Water & Wastewater | -790 | 0 |

JUSTIFICATION OF 2014 PROGRAM CHANGES

The Office of Insular Affairs (OIA) is not requesting funds for the Water and Wastewater program in 2014, a reduction of $790,000 and 0 FTE from the 2012 level. The funding level for the Water & Wastewater program in recent years only allows for the correction of smaller system deficiencies or temporary fixes such as the hiring of consultants. In 2014, pressing water and wastewater improvements will be addressed within existing Covenant capital improvement resources.

PROGRAM OVERVIEW

Improving water and wastewater systems in the territories is important as analyses conducted by local and Federal agencies have revealed deficiencies in the systems' abilities to meet environmental requirements. In the case of the U.S. Virgin Islands, inadequate wastewater treatment facilities have threatened health and reef environments and have culminated in court-ordered sanctions against the government. The CNMI remains the largest community in the United States without 24-hour potable water despite annual rainfall well in excess of double the national average. The water and wastewater needs of the islands will be addressed with Covenant capital improvement resources to address such deficiencies.

## 2014 PROGRAM PERFORMANCE

Although project proposals for 2013 Water & Wastewater funding have not yet been received, it is anticipated that the funds will be used to continue addressing critical water and wastewater needs in the territories in a similar fashion to previous years. The $790,000 in Water & Wastewater funding made available in 2012 is being used to address a critical project in Guam.

The Guam Waterworks Authority (GWA) was awarded $790,000 in 2012 for the Malojloj Line Water Booster Pump Station Upgrade project. The funding is being used to replace existing pumps with new energy efficient pumps and motors. The station is a critical facility to Guam's southern water system. The funding enables GWA to respond to a 2003 stipulated order to improve delivery of clean water and treatment of wastewater.

The Guam Waterworks Authority (GWA) was also awarded $525,000 in 2011 to rehabilitate the Barrigada Sewer Pump Station. The funding is being used to replace two sets of pumps and motors in the station, a critical part of Guam's wastewater system.

The CNMI's Commonwealth Utilities Corporation (CUC) was awarded $265,800 in 2011 to acquire additional professional services, including an electrical engineer and two engineering technicians, to assist CUC in complying with U.S. EPA water and wastewater standards and improve its water and wastewater programs.

7.

| Activity: | Territorial Assistance | | | | | |
| Subactivity: | Empowering Insular Communities $(000) | | | | | |

| | *2013 Full Yr. CR (PL 112-175)* | 2012 Enacted | 2014 | | | Change From 2012 (+/-) |
| | | | Fixed Costs & Related Changes (+/-) | Program Changes (+/-) | Budget Request | |
|---|---|---|---|---|---|---|
| Empowering Insular Communities | *2,218* | 2,205 | 0 | +766 | 2,971 | +766 |
| FTEs | *0* | 0 | 0 | 0 | 0 | 0 |

## SUMMARY OF 2014 PROGRAM CHANGES

| Request Component | | |
|---|---|---|
| | Amount | FTE |
| Empowering Insular Communities | +766 | 0 |

## JUSTIFICATION OF 2014 PROGRAM CHANGES

The 2014 budget request for the Empowering Insular Communities (EIC) program is $3.0 million and no FTE, a program increase of $766,000 with no change in FTE from the 2012 level.

## PROGRAM OVERVIEW

Insular communities face unique economic development challenges due to their geographic isolation, finite resources, and dependence on imported oil for their energy needs. To assist the islands in meeting these challenges, the Office of Insular Affairs is attempting to strengthen the foundations for economic development by addressing energy needs through building sustainable energy strategies that are not reliant on oil.

## 2014 PROGRAM PERFORMANCE

Sustainable Energy Strategies

Energy security is critical to the insular areas' future economic development and sustainability. In 2010, the Office of Insular Affairs (OIA) entered into an Inter-Agency Agreement (IAA) with the U.S. Department of Energy, National Renewable Energy Lab (NREL) to help develop long-term strategic energy plans in American Samoa, Commonwealth of the Northern Mariana Islands (CNMI), and Guam. In 2011, NREL provided the results of initial energy efficiency and renewable energy assessments and draft strategic energy plans for each of the three areas. Guam finalized its strategic energy plan in December 2012. NREL plans to work with American Samoa and the CNMI to finalize their plans in 2013.

NREL will then work with the territories to convert the energy assessment reports and strategic energy plans into detailed action plans. The action plans will establish specific goals, develop tasks to achieve these goals, assign responsibility for tasks, set deadlines and milestones, establish key performance indicators, develop a process for tracking progress, and identify the resources that will be needed to achieve the results. The action plans are to be completed by the end of September 2013. OIA plans to use the Empowering Insular Communities (EIC) funding to help the territories implement the actions identified in the strategic energy plans and action plans.

NREL has also been tasked with collecting energy baseline data and updating the data on an annual basis. Establishing a baseline and providing annual updates is fundamental to measuring OIA's performance goal of reducing the quantity of fuel used to produce a megawatt hour (MWh) of electricity. In 2011, NREL collected the 2010 energy data from the territorial utilities and integrated the data into a baseline tracking tool. NREL is behind schedule in collecting the 2011 and 2012 energy data and they hope to submit the updated data to OIA by March 31, 2013.

In fiscal year 2011, OIA awarded a total of $1.996 million in Empowering Insular Community (EIC) grant funding for renewable energy and energy efficiency projects. The University of Guam received a total of $900,000 to install rooftop solar arrays on its campus buildings to reduce the university's reliance on fossil fuels by 2 percent. The university plans to install at least three different types of photovoltaic systems and monitor the performance of the different systems in Guam's climate. NREL has provided technical support for the project by helping develop a scope of work and request for proposals. The university released the request for proposals in February 2013 and hopes to receive proposals by mid March.

NREL's "Commonwealth of the Northern Mariana Islands Initial Technical Assessment Report" identified the development of geothermal energy as a potential source of renewable energy if geothermal resources are discovered. OIA awarded a 2011 EIC grant in the amount of $500,000 to perform a geophysical survey in parallel with the Commonwealth Utilities Corporation's drilling of geothermal gradient holes. The geophysical survey will be useful in guiding geothermal gradient drilling and will shorten the time-table to exploration and development if results are favorable by facilitating the identification of exploration targets. The Commonwealth Utilities Corporation is currently going through the process of procuring a contractor to drill test holes in the Gualo Rai area of Saipan. If significant heat is found at the appropriate depth, they will conduct geophysical testing on the surface to further determine if it can be developed into geothermal energy.

OIA awarded a 2011 EIC grant in the amount of $596,000 to the American Samoa Power Authority for various renewable energy and conservation projects. OIA recently approved a scope of work for $206,000 of the total to be used to perform a grid integration study. A grid integration study is a critical step as American Samoa seeks to add more renewable energy to its power grid. The remainder of the funding will support a recycling rebate program and prepaid meters for the Manu'a Islands.

In 2012, OIA awarded a total of $1.085 million in EIC grant funding for renewable energy and energy efficiency projects that were in accordance with Guam's draft Strategic Energy Plan. The Guam Power Authority (GPA) received a total of $505,000 in EIC funding to support the implementation of a wind turbine pilot project in the Cotal area of Guam. The EIC grant supplements a 2009 Capital Improvement Project grant OIA awarded for $1 million for the installation of the 275 kW wind turbine. GPA is currently developing a request for proposals and exploring ways to address the social readiness and acceptance of wind energy on the island.

The Guam Department of Administration's General Services Agency received a 2012 EIC grant for $250,000 for the installation of rooftop photovoltaic solar panels, energy-efficient air-conditioners, windows, doors, lights, and a "cool rooftop." The General Services Agency is currently developing a request for proposals for the project. The photovoltaic system will be tied to the grid system thereby allowing all excess power generated to be fed back into the power grid.

In 2012, OIA awarded a $180,000 EIC grant to the Guam Department of Public Works (DPW) for an important energy efficiency project. The funding will be used to replace 87 windows and 37 doors at DPW buildings with energy star-rated hardware.

The Guam Energy Office received a 2012 EIC grant for $150,000 to partner with a trades institution that will develop the energy code curriculum to train building industry professionals of the importance of following Guam's recently developed Tropical Energy Code. This project was identified in Guam's "Initial Technical Assessment Report" as high priority among energy efficiency projects.

Public Safety Equipment
Of the $2.2 million appropriated for 2012, $1.12 million was awarded to the Guam Fire Department to purchase needed public safety equipment. The Guam Fire Department is currently developing specifications for the equipment in preparation for the procurement process.

- $600,000      Fire Ladder Truck
- $240,000      Two Rescue Trucks
- $280,000      Rigid Hull Inflatable Rescue Boat & Equipment

8.

| Activity: | **Territorial Assistance** | | | | | |
|---|---|---|---|---|---|---|
| Subactivity: | **Compact Impact - Discretionary** $(000) | | | | | |
| | | | 2014 | | | |
| | *2013 Full Yr. CR (PL 112-175)* | **2012 Enacted** | **Fixed Costs & Related Changes (+/-)** | **Program Changes (+/-)** | **Budget Request** | **Change from 2012 (+/-)** |
| | *5,000* | [4,992*] | 0 | -1,992 | 3,000 | -1,992 |
| FTEs | *0* | 0 | 0 | 0 | 0 | 0 |

*Funded in General Technical Assistance

## SUMMARY OF 2014 PROGRAM CHANGES

| **Request Component** | | |
|---|---|---|
| Program Changes | Amount | FTE |
| Compact Impact - Discretionary | -1,992 | 0 |

## JUSTIFICATION OF 2014 PROGRAM CHANGES

The 2014 budget request for discretionary Compact Impact funding is $3.0 million, a program decrease of $2.0 million, and 0 FTE, funded in General Technical Assistance for Compact Impact in 2012. Discretionary Compact Impact grants funds will be awarded in conjunction with other currently authorized mandatory grants to help offset educational costs incurred by jurisdictions that are affected by Compact migration, as authorized by section 104(e) of Public Law 108-188.

## PROGRAM OVERVIEW

Discretionary Compact Impact grants supplement the $30.0 million permanently appropriated for Compact Impact as authorized by Section 104(e) of Title One of the amended Compacts of Free Association. However, discretionary Compact Impact funding can only be used to offset educational service and infrastructure costs incurred by the affected jurisdictions due to the residence of qualified nonimmigrants from the Republic of the Marshall Islands, the Federated States of Micronesia, or the Republic of Palau.

*Description of Compact Impact - Permanent*

Section 104 (e) of Title One of the amended Compacts of Free Association describes the financial assistance committed by the United States to the State of Hawaii, Guam, the Commonwealth of the Northern Mariana Islands and American Samoa. The goal of this financial support is to provide through 2023, $30.0 million in grants to affected jurisdictions to aid in defraying costs incurred as a result of increased demands placed on health, educational, social, or public sector services, or infrastructure related to such services, due to the residence of qualified nonimmigrants from the Republic of the Marshall Islands, the Federated States of Micronesia, or the Republic of Palau.

The $30.0 million distribution is based on a ratio allocation to the government of each affected jurisdiction on the basis of the results of the most recent enumeration. At a minimum, enumerations will be conducted every five years. The most recent enumeration was completed in 2009 by the U.S. Census Bureau and the results were used to determine the distribution of the $30.0 million beginning in 2010. This allocation is in accordance with the provision in Section 104(e)(5) of Title One of the amended Compacts of Free Association.

## 2014 PROGRAM PERFORMANCE

Like permanently appropriated Compact Impact, discretionary Compact Impact funding will be distributed amongst the affected jurisdictions based on a ratio allocation to the government of each affected jurisdiction on the basis of the results of the most recent enumeration, that of 2009. Compact Impact funding can only be used to offset educational service and infrastructure costs incurred by the affected jurisdictions due to the residence of qualified nonimmigrants from the Republic of the Marshall Islands, the Federated States of Micronesia, or the Republic of Palau.

American Samoa received $3,000 in discretionary Compact Impact funding in 2012 for the operational needs of the Nursing Program at the American Samoa Community College. The funding will be used for training materials and equipment to assist in the education of nursing students at the college. Although OIA has not yet received a 2013 spending plan from American Samoa, it is anticipated that the funds will be used in a manner similar to 2012.

The CNMI received an additional $320,999 in 2012 for discretionary Compact Impact funding and applied it to educational services at the Public School System and the Northern Marianas College. In 2013, under an annualized continuing resolution level, the CNMI would receive $321,500.

In 2012, Guam received an additional $2,800,000 in discretionary Compact Impact funding for the Guam Department of Education. At the annualized continuing resolution level in 2013, Guam would receive $2,804,500 for education Compact Impact.

# Compacts of Free Association

## D. Compacts of Free Association

1.

| Activity: | Compact of Free Association (Current Appropriation) | | | | | |
|---|---|---|---|---|---|---|
| Subactivity: | Federal Services Assistance   $(000) | | | | | |
| | | | **2014** | | | |
| | *2013 Full Yr. CR (PL 112-175)* | **2012 Enacted** | **Fixed Costs & Related Changes (+/-)** | **Program Changes (+/-)** | **Budget Request** | **Change from 2012 (+/-)** |
| | *2,831* | 2,814 | 0 | +4 | 2,818 | +4 |
| FTEs | *0* | 0 | 0 | 0 | 0 | 0 |

## SUMMARY OF 2014 PROGRAM CHANGES

| Request Component | | |
|---|---|---|
| Program Changes | Amount | FTE |
| Federal Services Assistance | +4 | 0 |

## JUSTIFICATION OF 2014 PROGRAM CHANGES

The 2014 budget request for Federal Services Assistance is $2.8 million, a program increase of $4,000 with no change in FTE from the 2012 level.

## PROGRAM OVERVIEW

The Compacts of Free Association guarantee that the freely associated states (FAS) will continue to receive certain Federal services in accordance with negotiated agreements, as is the case for the Federated States of Micronesia (FSM) and the Republic of the Marshall Islands (RMI). These services include those of the U.S. Postal Service (USPS).

The United States Postal Service (USPS) provides transportation of mail to and from the freely associated states. Although the freely associated state governments operate their own postal services for internal mail distribution, they have almost no role in the international movement of mail. By agreement, U.S. postal rates are the floors for rates charged by the FAS. U.S. domestic first class postage rates were formerly in effect for mail from the United States to the FAS. Current agreements with the FSM and RMI allow phased increases to reach established international rates. The FAS operate the local post offices and transport mail to and from air and seaports. All proceeds from the sale of FAS stamps and postal indicia are retained by the FAS governments.

The effectiveness of the USPS program, especially for the Republic of the Marshall Islands, is dependent on the availability of commercial air service. To maintain mail service, the USPS in recent years has chartered special flights and purchased additional space on passenger flights to transport mail. The total cost of this service exceeds the subsidy requested by OIA. The additional costs are paid by USPS from its revenues.

## 2014 PROGRAM PERFORMANCE

OIA will enter into a reimbursable agreement with the USPS for services provided to the FAS.

2.

| Activity: | Compact of Free Association (Current Appropriation) | | | | | |
|---|---|---|---|---|---|---|
| Subactivity: | Enewetak  $(000) | | | | | |
| | | | 2014 | | | |
| | *2013 Full Yr. CR (PL 112-175)* | 2012 Enacted | Fixed Costs & Related Changes (+/-) | Program Changes (+/-) | Budget Request | Change from 2012 (+/-) |
| | *502* | 499 | 0 | -263 | 236 | -263 |
| FTEs | *0* | 0 | 0 | 0 | 0 | 0 |

## SUMMARY OF 2014 PROGRAM CHANGES

| Request Component | | |
|---|---|---|
| Program Changes | Amount | FTE |
| Enewetak | -263 | 0 |

## JUSTIFICATION OF 2014 PROGRAM CHANGES

The 2014 budget request for the Enewetak program is $236,000 and no FTE, a program decrease of $263,000 and no change in FTE from the 2012 level. At the 2014 request level, OIA will decrease supplemental discretionary funding for the Enewetak Support program. The program will operate at a reduced level using the remaining $236,000 in discretionary funding to supplement the $1.3 million in permanent funding, with adjustment for inflation, provided under the amended Compact of Free Association (Public Law 108-188).

## PROGRAM OVERVIEW

The natural vegetation of Enewetak Atoll was largely destroyed during World War II and during the subsequent nuclear testing program conducted by the United States. Following the cleanup and resettlement of Enewetak, food bearing trees and root crops had to be replanted. However, the depleted soil of the island environment made it difficult to support sufficient agricultural activity to feed the population. In 1980, the Enewetak Support program was implemented to provide supplemental foods for the community, replant vegetation of the inhabited islands, provide agricultural maintenance training and transport food to the island.

The Enewetak community developed a plan with the assistance of the University of the South Pacific to provide greater amounts of locally produced food and to better integrate necessary imported food into the local diets. A continuing effort is being made to replenish the atoll's soil and agricultural potential. The replanted vegetation is producing at pre-nuclear testing period levels, when the population was about 150 people, but is not sufficient for the current population of about 800 people.

## 2014 PROGRAM PERFORMANCE

The Enewetak program currently uses approximately 40 percent of its funding for operations of the agriculture field station and the agriculture rehabilitation program. Approximately 31 percent of the funding is used to purchases food and commodities for the residents of the atoll. The remaining funds are used to operate the atoll's new vessel and support office in Majuro. OIA will provide grants for Enewetak in 2014 to continue these activities.

3.

| Activity: | Compact of Free Association (Current Appropriation) | | | | | |
| Subactivity: | Palau Compact Extension   $(000) | | | | | |
| | | | 2014 | | | |
| | 2013 Full Yr. CR (PL 112-175) | 2012 Enacted | Fixed Costs & Related Changes (+/-) | Program Changes (+/-) | Budget Request | Change from 2012 (+/-) |
| | 13,147 | 13,147 | 0 | -13,147 | 0 | -13,147 |
| FTEs | 0 | 0 | 0 | 0 | 0 | 0 |

## SUMMARY OF 2014 PROGRAM CHANGES

| Request Component | | |
|---|---|---|
| Program Changes | Amount | FTE |
| Palau Compact Extension | -13,147 | 0 |

## JUSTIFICATION OF 2014 PROGRAM CHANGES

The 2014 budget request does not fund another Palau Compact Extension, a decrease of $13.2 million and no change in FTE from the 2012 level.

Economic assistance provisions under Palau's Compact of Free Association (P.L. 99-658) expired at the end of 2009. The Department of the Interior, Environment, and Related Agencies Appropriations Act, 2010 (P.L. 111-88 Sec. 122) and subsequent continuing appropriations acts have continued to extend economic assistance to Palau.

On February 14, 2011, S. 343 was introduced in the Senate seeking to continue the U.S. Compact financial relationship with the Republic of Palau. The proposed bill would provide $250 million in financial assistance to the Republic of Palau through 2024. The bill has not been enacted by the U.S. Congress to date. The goals of the continued funding are to maintain the viability of Palau's trust fund and to keep government spending stable while Palau enacts policy reforms to strengthen its economy.

As a result of the Senate introducing S. 343, OIA is not seeking current funds for the Palau Compact Extension in 2014.

## PROGRAM OVERVIEW

Economic assistance provisions under Palau's Compact of Free Association (P.L. 99-658) were set to expire at the end of 2009. The Department of the Interior, Environment, and Related Agencies Appropriations Act, 2010 (Pub. L. No. 111-88 Sec. 122) and subsequent continuing appropriations acts have continued to extend economic assistance to Palau within OIA current budget authority.

## 2014 PROGRAM PERFORMANCE

2013 Palau Compact Extension funding will be administered as it was under the Compact according to the Fiscal Procedures Agreement for the Republic of Palau.

4.

| Account: | Compact of Free Association (Permanent and Indefinite) | | | | | |
|---|---|---|---|---|---|---|
| Activity: | Economic Assistance | | | | | |
| Subactivity: | Federated States of Micronesia and Republic of the Marshall Islands $(000) | | | | | |

| | | | 2014 | | | |
|---|---|---|---|---|---|---|
| | *2013 Full Yr. CR (PL 112-175)* | **2012 Enacted** | Fixed Costs & Related Changes (+/-) | Program Changes (+/-) | Budget Request | Change from 2012 (+/-) |
| RMI | *68,090* | 66,839 | 0 | +8,407 | 75,246 | +8,407 |
| FSM | *106,663* | 104,984 | 0 | +4,045 | 109,029 | +4,045 |
| Judicial Training | *347* | 340 | 0 | +13 | 353 | +13 |
| Total | *175,100* | 172,163 | **0** | **+12,465** | **184,628** | **+12,465** |
| FTEs | *0* | 0 | 0 | 0 | 0 | 0 |

## SUMMARY OF 2014 PROGRAM CHANGES

| Request Component | | |
|---|---|---|
| Program Changes | Amount | FTE |
| RMI | +8,407 | 0 |
| FSM | +4,045 | 0 |
| Judicial Training | +13 | 0 |

## JUSTIFICATION OF 2014 PROGRAM CHANGES

The 2014 budget request for Compact of Free Association - Economic Assistance to the Marshall Islands and Federated States of Micronesia is $184.6 million, an increase of $12.5 million with no additional FTEs from the 2012 enacted level. The program changes in this account are required inflation adjustments under the amended Compact of Free Association. The increases are based on changes in the United States Gross Domestic Product Implicit Price Deflator but may not exceed 5% annually.

## PROGRAM OVERVIEW

Article I of Title Two of the Compacts of Free Association describes the financial assistance commitment by the United States to the Federated States of Micronesia (FSM) and the Republic of the Marshall Islands (RMI). The first period of financial assistance expired on September 30, 2003. Following four years of negotiations led by the Department of State with support from OIA, Congress enacted amendments to the Compact as Public Law 108-188. These amendments also include a new permanent and indefinite appropriation that ensures continuation of direct financial assistance through 2023.

The long term goal of United States' Compact financial support is to assist the freely associated states "in their efforts to advance the economic self-sufficiency of their peoples." The funding provided over the past seventeen years provided the basis for meeting the two primary political goals of the compact, to (1) secure self-government for each country by ending the four decades-old Trusteeship; and (2) ensure national security rights for the United States in the freely associated states. The two primary goals could not have been achieved without the stability compact funding gave the FSM and RMI economies.

The first Compact financial assistance period and related agreements provided funding by category and purpose, and established general guidelines for the use of funds. The local governments, through their own legal processes, allocated funding among self-chosen priorities. Compact funds were disbursed to the FSM and RMI according to negotiated procedures rather than standard Federal practices. All funds dedicated to capital purposes were transferred to the governments the first day of the fiscal year. All operational funding was disbursed in quarterly lump sums. Customary regulations for the use of Federal funds, such as the Common Rule for grant funds, did not apply to Compact funding. The lack of effective enforcement mechanisms over the use of funds was well documented. This was, however, by design. The Compact was consciously negotiated to limit U.S. control over funding given to the newly established democracies.

During the first Compact period, the FSM and the RMI did not make significant progress toward achieving the long-term Compact goals of self-sufficiency. The U.S. believes part of the reason for poor economic performance over the past seventeen years was in the design of the first Compact itself. The lack of performance standards, measures and monitoring systems allowed poor practices to take root in local government administration.

The amended Compact provides assistance in the form of direct grants in six sectors: education, health care, infrastructure, public sector capacity building, private sector development, and environment. Joint economic management committees, comprised of high ranking officials from the U.S. and the RMI or FSM, meet no less than annually to agree on the allocation of Compact funds among the sectors and to discuss performance, accountability issues and conditions for the use of assistance. OIA serves as the administrator of the financial assistance and ensures enforcement of conditions. An office for monitoring Compact assistance has been established in Honolulu and personnel have also been located in the RMI and FSM capitals. Through a negotiated fiscal procedures agreement, accountability and control standards similar to those which apply domestically to grant agreements between the Federal Government and State and local governments have been implemented.

The amended Compact also requires the United States to make contributions to trust funds for each government. The trust funds are intended to help provide a base for financial self-sufficiency following the conclusion of direct assistance in 2023.

## 2014 PROGRAM PERFORMANCE

OIA will continue to monitor activities in the FSM and the RMI through a combination of site-visits and quarterly review of FSM and RMI-submitted financial and performance reports. It is expected office staff will:

- Conduct a minimum of 200 (-20% from 2011) person-days of site visits in the RMI and FSM.
- Collect quantitative and qualitative data on performance objectives and measures.
- Issue and administer all sector grants and the Supplemental Education Grant in the RMI and FSM.
- Convene regular and special meetings of the joint economic management and financial accountability committee for the RMI and the joint economic management committee for the FSM to address major issues as they arise.

Specific information for 2014 is not available at the time of this report due to the nature of the Compact agreement. As agreed to in the Compact, performance plans and budgets for 2014 are not submitted by the FSM and RMI until 90 days before the start of the fiscal year. However, a brief summary of 2013 program performance information for the FSM and RMI sector grants is provided on the next few pages.

**i. Fiscal Year 2013 Sector Allocations for the FSM**

The following is a breakdown of grant allocations to the FSM by sector:

| Sector | Funds Allocated |
| --- | --- |
| Education | $28,034,838 |
| Health | $20,692,562 |
| Capacity Building | $2,946,227 |
| Private Sector | $2,373,494 |
| Environment | $1,718,017 |
| Enhanced Reporting & Accountability | $1,481,237 |
| Infrastructure | $24,437,952 |
| **Total** | **$81,684,327** |

Education

FSM states have aligned their goals with the following four education goals cited in the FSM Strategic Development Plan:

1. Improve the quality of instructional services to early childhood, elementary and secondary education.
2. Improve the quality of education services and programs.
3. Meet the manpower needs of the nation.
4. Allow FSM students to compete in postsecondary education to assist in the economic and social development of the FSM.

The Compact, Supplemental Education Grants, and Special Education funds from the US Department of Education continue to provide over 90% of the budget for Education in the FSM. The FSM has 193 schools – 133 elementary, 21 secondary, 25 Early Childhood Education Centers (ECE), and 14 schools with primary through secondary grades. About a third of these schools are located on remote outer islands more than 200 miles from the population centers of the four states and accessible primarily through a handful of largely unreliable ships. The ECE-12 system serves 28,845 students which is about 78% of the total school-aged population.

The geographic isolation of these schools, lack of resources and access to technology, and a limited pool of qualified human resources are major impediments to providing quality education service. As Compact funding continues to decline in real value, states, which are responsible for operating schools, will face even greater challenges to improve education service delivery.

At least half of the FSM's student population tested in the nation's National Minimum Competency Test (NMCT) is performing below the competency level expected for their grades. Most students enrolling in the College of Micronesia spend about one year in remedial courses. The Joint Economic Management Committee (JEMCO) has recommended that the FSM prioritize improving student performance in the primary and secondary level. More specifically, JEMCO recommended that more Compact funds be allocated for the improvement of results in the NMCT, full implementation of the FSM School Accreditation System, and Teacher/Principal Professional Development and Certification.

In its FY 2013 budget, the FSM allocated more resources to the three identified initiatives and some improvements are being realized. Nationwide, a remaining 20% of teachers are without college degrees (10% reduction from 2011 and 45% from 2008) and the country is on track to decrease that percentage further. The FSM has also developed a more rigorous testing and accreditation program so that all schools receiving Compact funding are tested on the NMCT and evaluated as part of the FSM School Accreditation System.

Health

In 2013, the FSM received a Compact health sector grant of $20.69 million. As has been the case historically, health sector grant funding primarily supported regular recurring operations of the four state in-patient facilities.

The allotments were:

| | |
|---|---|
| Chuuk State | $ 8,608,714 |
| Kosrae State | $ 2,111,506 |
| Pohnpei State | $ 5,768,196 |
| Yap State | $ 3,308,441 |
| National Government | $ 895,705 |

All four states complied with JEMCO's resolution requiring funding support for three health initiatives: decreasing recurring diabetes-related hospitalizations, eliminating leprosy, and preventing and controlling Multiple Drug Resistant Tuberculosis. The budget levels proposed by Yap and Kosrae were adequate as were their plans. Chuuk, however, did not budget sufficiently for all of its MDR TB and NCD (non-communicable disease) activities. Consequently, it committed to address these shortfalls internally as best it can. Pohnpei State found it necessary to decrease the level of Compact funding for off island medical referrals in order to support its three health initiatives.

The annual reduction (decrement) in available financial assistance for the Compact's six sectors has had a profound effect on health care delivery. Although health continues to be second only to education as a priority for Compact support, allocations for all four FSM state health departments have flat-lined or declined. The resulting trend of budget decline, congestion, and ad hoc cuts will continue unabated until the states find workable alternatives to offset the loss of Compact dollars and the health departments earnestly implement programs that trim inefficient and ineffective activities and raise fees for service.

## The FY 2013 JEMCO Request

The Government of the Federated States of Micronesia (FSM) requested a total of $20,692,562 in Compact health sector grant funding for FY 2013. The proposed amount disregards inflationary costs in pharmaceutical supplies, transportation, shipping and POL, and is best characterized as maintenance of effort. It leaves little maneuverability for innovation and growth. Even the phrase "maintenance of effort" is a misnomer. The exclusion of an inflation index and the recurring lack of money for regular medical equipment replacements and upgrades and maintenance from FY 2004 and on, implies that health has lost considerable ground.

Shown below are the allocation levels for the four state governments and for the National Department of Health and Social Affairs (DHSA):

| Sub-Allottee | Total Compact Dollars | Proposed Grant Amount | Proportional Share Health Sector Grant | Service Delivery Responsibility |
|---|---|---|---|---|
| Chuuk State | $30,954,739 | $ 8,608,714 | 28% | Direct Care |
| Kosrae State | $ 8,879,123 | $ 2,111,506 | 24% | Direct Care |
| Pohnpei State | $20,617,486 | $ 5,768,196 | 28% | Direct Care |
| Yap State | $12,862,509 | $ 3,308,441 | 26% | Direct Care |
| National Government | $ 8,145,984 | $   895,705 | 11% | Indirect/National Policy |
| Total | $81,459,840 | $20,692,562 | 100% | |

The share of health dollars going to the FSM's four state governments does not follow the country's internal revenue distribution formula; instead, each state receives an overall Compact allotment from the National Government and then, within that amount, determines its health sector grant budget. Funding reflects internal state priorities and competing demands for shrinking support.

**JEMCO Mandated Health Initiatives:** All four FSM state health departments complied with *JEMCO 2012-MT-5*, requiring adequate funding in FY 2013 for MDR TB/TB prevention and control, leprosy elimination, and the reduction of recurring diabetes-related hospitalizations. The resolution ensures that Pohnpei and Chuuk continue the important activities begun in the current fiscal year and enjoins Kosrae and Yap to improve their prevention and management efforts as well. (JEMCO's approval of health sector grants for FY 2014 through 2017 will be contingent on similar budgetary support for the three initiatives.)

| | Reduce Diabetic Hospitalizations | | Eliminate Leprosy | | Prevent/Control MDR TB and TB | |
|---|---|---|---|---|---|---|
| | 2012 | 2013 | 2012 | 2013 | 2012 | 2013 |
| **CHUUK** | | | | | | |
| **TOTAL** | **$53,271** | **$166,367** | **$243,000** | **$125,754** | **$28,912** | **$335,176** |
| *Compact* | *$34,499* | *$147,595* | *$243,000* | *$125,754* | *$259,000* | *$304,984* |
| *Federal* | | | | | | |
| *Grant* | *$18,772* | *$ 18,772* | - | - | *$ 30,912* | *$ 30,192* |
| **KOSRAE** | | | | | | |
| **TOTAL** | NA | **$52,038** | NA | **$2,600** | NA | **$25,320** |
| *Compact* | - | *$33,638* | - | *$2,600* | - | *$3,040* |
| *Federal* | | | | | | |
| *Grant* | *$15,710* | *$18,400* | - | - | *$10,917* | *$22,280* |
| **POHNPEI** | | | | | | |
| **TOTAL** | **$77,610** | **$83,150** | **$81,400** | **$66,000** | **$37,596** | **$90,796** |
| *Compact* | *$64,900* | *$71,000* | *$81,400* | *$66,000* | - | *$53,200* |
| *Federal* | | | | | | |
| *Grant* | *$12,710* | *$12,150* | - | - | *$37,596* | *$37,596* |
| **YAP** | | | | | | |
| **TOTAL** | **$16,200** | **$34,570** | NA | **$15,891** | NA | **$39,945** |
| *Compact* | - | *$18,500* | - | *$15,891* | - | *$16,000* |
| *Federal* | | | | | | |
| *Grant* | *$16,200* | *$16,070* | - | - | *$23,945* | *$23,945* |

Although all four budgets earmark funds for JEMCO's three mandatory initiatives, Chuuk's budget significantly overlooked MDR-TB staff overtime, hazard pay, the purchase of preventive drugs, and POL for community DOT and contact tracing.

Chuuk's activities to prevent recurring diabetes related hospitalizations also lacked sufficient resources. The proposal did not include funds to obtain a variety of appropriate exercise equipment for its wellness center, and neglected funding to compensate health counselors (well-controlled diabetics who will voluntarily provide inpatient counseling) and initiate mandatory patient teaching prior to discharge. Chuuk must either find $40,000 within its FY 2013 budget or scale back on program plans.

Pohnpei's compliance meant a $190,200 reduction in off-island referral funding to make available Compact funding for its three continuing initiatives. The offset, while protecting the performance progress of primary care and prevention activities, newly risks a sharp contraction in medically necessary referrals to Manila hospitals. It may spur Pohnpei's hospital to tighten its referral policy and practices, and expand in-house medical diagnostics and therapies; however, given the health department's shrinking budget, any increase in internal capacity will be possible only to the extent that new funding becomes available.

**Compact Funding of Medical Referral Operations in Honolulu:** The budgets of the four health departments complied with *JEMCO 2012-MT-6*, a resolution that excludes operating costs for Honolulu-based medical referral coordination and patient housing from Compact funding support.

Grant Compliance

JEMCO stipulated that Compact funding allocated to the FSM National Department of Health and Social Affairs in FY 2012 link expenditures to strategic activities. The proposed budget for FY 2013 continued this activity-based arrangement:

## FY 2013 DHSA Activity-Based Proposal
### Total Cost: $895,705

| Activity Clusters | Personnel | Travel | Contractual | OCE | Fixed Assets | Totals |
|---|---|---|---|---|---|---|
| HEALTH SYSTEMS SUPPORT | | | | | | |
| 1. Minimum standards of management | $26,043 | $11,536 | - | $7,417 | - | $44,996 |
| 2. Sustainable community mapping | $26,043 | $24,000 | - | $7,417 | - | $57,460 |
| 3. Clinical standards of care | $26,042 | $40,000 | - | $7,417 | - | $73,459 |
| 4. Minimum standards for health facilities | $26,042 | $ 8,000 | - | $7,417 | - | $41,459 |
| 5. Specialized off-island medical teams | - | - | $200,000 | - | - | $200,000 |
| 6. Regional pathologist/laboratory | - | - | $100,000 | - | - | $100,000 |
| 7. Evaluation of performance indicators | - | $6,000 | $16,000 | - | - | $22,000 |
| Cluster Sub-total | $104,170 | $89,536 | $316,000 | $29,668 | - | $539,374 |
| FOOD SAFETY INSPECTION/ANALYTICAL SERV. | | | | | | |
| 1. Strengthen inspection services | $154,130 | $5,751 | $8,190 | $18,060 | - | $186,13 |
| 2. Strengthen analysis capacity | $25,000 | $10,000 | $25,000 | $15,000 | $15,000 | $90,000 |
| 3. Review food safety legislation | - | $5,158 | - | - | - | $5,158 |
| 4. Strengthen food safety training | - | $15,972 | - | - | - | $15,972 |
| Cluster Sub-total | $179,130 | $36,881 | $33,190 | $33,060 | $15,000 | $297,261 |
| ENVIRONMENTAL HEALTH SERVICES | | | | | | |
| 1. Develop laws and regulations (NEW) | - | $20,820 | $20,000 | $18,250 | - | $59,070 |
| Cluster Sub-total | | $20,820 | $20,000 | $18,250 | - | $59,070 |
| DHSA EXPENSE CATEGORIES TOTAL | $283,300 | $147,237 | $369,190 | $80,978 | $15,000 | $895,705 |

DHSA's FY 2013 cluster of activities relating to food safety maintains the day-to-day functions of its environmental health division. The health systems support cluster continues efforts to develop standards of care and sustainable methods to map community needs for a second year. These activities are not supplemental but are part-and-parcel of DHSA's constitutionally mandated role. Other continuing budgeted activities include bringing in specialty medical teams and supporting the regional pathology laboratory effort. DHSA's one new health systems support activity earmarks funding to implement an evaluation of performance indicators and data.

### Health Budgets in Jeopardy

The annual reduction in available financial assistance for the Compact's six sectors has a profound effect on health care delivery. Although health continues to be second only to education as a priority for Compact support, allocations for all four FSM state health departments have flat-lined or declined. The smaller budgets have created an unintended result; that is, the need to cover personnel expenses and rapidly rising utility costs have "crowded out" other important recurring needs such as housekeeping and facilities maintenance, POL, interisland travel by mobile teams, and medical equipment. Staff development and continuing education, both critical elements in maintaining a competent health workforce, have virtually disappeared from state budgets.

This trend of budget decline, congestion, and ad hoc cuts will continue unabated until the states find workable alternatives to offset the loss of Compact dollars and the health departments earnestly implement programs that trim inefficient and ineffective activities and raise fees for service.

The Compact still finances nearly 100% of the operating budgets of the four FSM states. Ironically, Pohnpei is the only state that appropriates general funds to its health department, yet its health budget has been the most volatile and lacking in all the FSM. This dependence on shrinking Compact dollars is paralyzing. It jeopardizes improvements already made in the delivery of health services, not just in Pohnpei but in the other states as well. It affects, too, their ability to mobilize health services in the face of public health emergencies, as Yap can attest as it grappled with dengue last year and again this year and as Chuuk can as it continues to cope with MDR-TB.

Sustaining improvements and the status quo is difficult enough but the biggest challenge that the states will face in FY 2013 and onward is the deterioration in the quality, not the quantity of basic health programs and services.

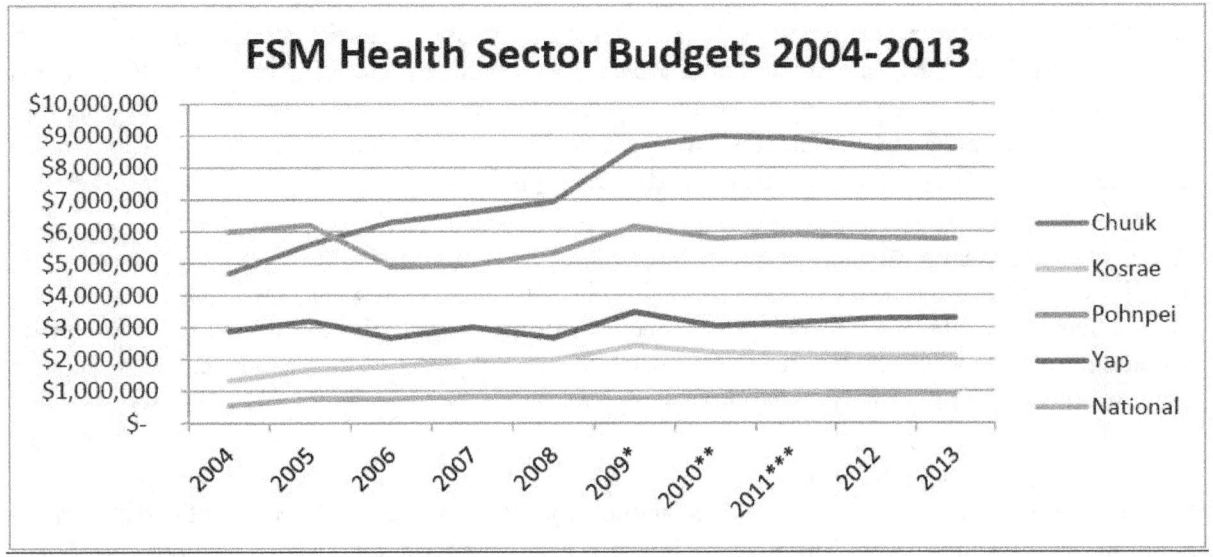

## Public Infrastructure
Approximately $228 million of Compact Public Sector Infrastructure assistance has been made available to the FSM from October 2003 to present. To-date, $133 million has been obligated for project construction and construction administration and management. Approximately $95 million remains unobligated under the Infrastructure sector.

The FSM received a public sector infrastructure allocation of $24.2 million during 2013. This funding will be obligated for individual projects when design and engineering phases are complete. The FSM National Government's Infrastructure Program Management Unit (PMU) currently has approximately 6 projects in various stages of design. Six new elementary school buildings have been completed in

Pohnpei. A $26.2 million water, sewer, road and drainage project in Weno, Chuuk is approximately 80% complete with a revised targeted completion date of November 2013. Construction of early childhood education and post-secondary facilities continued in Yap State. Two elementary school buildings have been completed in Kosrae State.

The main obstacle to steady implementation of the infrastructure sector is that the FSM has been unable to ensure professional management and effectiveness of the $24 million per year program on an ongoing basis.

Public Sector Capacity Building
In 2013, the FSM received $2.9 million for the capacity building sector. Fiscal Year 2013 continued the successful articulation regarding the uses of funding started in Fiscal Year 2012. Clear deliverables and activities are specified in program-oriented proposals. The FSM has not yet developed a medium-term plan to guide how the sector grant may be optimally utilized in order to achieve measurable public sector capacity building gains.

Environment
In 2013, the FSM received an allocation of approximately $16 million for its environment sector. Each State received funding for an Environmental Protection Agency or similar agency with a like mission. Financial assistance also supported marine and forestry conservation efforts. Public education programs were a part of all programs funded under this sector. The lack of national goals for the environment sector continued to hamper the evaluation of performance progress.

Private Sector Development
In 2013, the FSM received an allocation of $2.3 million for its private sector development sector grant. This amount funded the basic operations of a number of different agencies to increase tourism, promote agriculture, and support small businesses. The lack of national goals for the private sector development sector grant continued to hamper the evaluation of performance progress.

Enhanced Reporting and Accountability
In 2013, the FSM received a grant of $1.4 million for the newly created sector entitled "Enhanced Reporting and Accountability." This sector is intended to address the additional complexities and costs of compliance inherent in the Compact, as amended, specifically those related to budgeting, financial accountability, and expanded financial and performance reporting requirements.

Priorities are given to achieving and maintaining full and timely compliance with Articles V and VI of this Agreement, the development and operation of a Financial Management Information System that is capable of accurately and efficiently accounting for and reporting on the use of Compact and all other funds available to the national and state governments of the Federated States of Micronesia; the development and operation of a performance-based budgeting and reporting system for the planned use and expenditure of Compact and all other funds available to each of the national and state governments of the Federated States of Micronesia; and including the development and operation of financial management procedures, practices and internal controls that ensure timely revenue collections, accurate and timely payments, and accurate and timely submission of all required quarterly and annual reports by each of the national and state governments of the Federated States of Micronesia.

## ii. Fiscal Year 2013 Sector Allocations for the RMI

The following is a breakdown of grant allocations to the RMI by sector and Compact of Free Association, Section 211-mandated funding:

| Sector | Funds Allocated |
|---|---|
| Education | $11,598,952 |
| Health | $6,693,788 |
| Infrastructure | $9,406,891 |
| Environment | $325,000 |
| Ebeye Special Needs | $3,587,010 |
| Kwajalein Environmental Impact | $231,420 |
| RMI Trust Fund | $ 13,306,650 |
| Kwajalein landowner Payments | $17,356,500 |
| Disaster Assistance Emergency Fund | $458,200 |
| RMI Single Audit (FY12) | $ 500,000 |
| Kwajalein Impact Fund | $1,275,000 |
| **Total** | **$64,739,411** |

Education
The RMI is using Compact education sector funds to make progress in meeting the following education goals:

1. Improve curriculum at all levels.
2. Improve effectiveness of staff and teachers.
3. Improve student performance and learning outcomes.
4. Implement infrastructure development and maintenance plan.
5. Supplement special educational needs of Ebeye.
6. Provide financial assistance to post-secondary students.
7. Improve performance of the College of the Marshall Islands.

Compact, Ebeye Special Needs (ESN), Supplemental Education Grants, and Special Education funds from the US Department of Education fund 75% of RMI's education system. In School Year 2011-2012, over 15,000 students were enrolled in 95 elementary and 16 secondary schools including non-public schools which receive financial assistance from the Ministry of Education (MOE). Many of these schools are located on remote atolls over 200 miles from the population centers and accessible only by ship. The geographic isolation of these schools, lack of resources and access to technology, and a limited pool of qualified human resources are major impediments to providing quality education service. As Compact funding continues to decline in real value, MOE will face even greater challenges to improve education service delivery.

Lack of credentialed teachers and low student achievement continue to be associated and persistent problems. About 40% of RMI's teachers still possess only a high school degree. Over the past five years, the RMI has allocated over $2.5 million dollars to upgrade its teachers' credentials. Despite this significant investment, the percentage of teachers with only a high school degree has remained roughly the same due to high turnover rates. Many teachers leave for higher paying government jobs once they have received a college degree. As more teachers receive college degrees and a commensurate increase in their salary, personnel costs will rise to unsustainable levels if there is no contribution of additional resources to MOE's budget.

Under the new leadership, MOE has set the following actions to improve education in the RMI:
1. Achieve an annual 5% improvement in student performance and in student and teacher attendance levels for every school.
2. Have all students able to read in both English and Marshallese by third grade by 2015.
3. Provide vocational and other life skills for students not able to enter high school and college.
4. Establish a new school accreditation system.

Health
For FY 2013, the Ministry of Health identified adequate resources for the three special initiatives required by JEMFAC; that is, the continuation of leprosy elimination and MDR TB prevention and management activities, and the institution of steps to reduce recurring diabetes-related hospitalizations.

The Ministry of Health combined a number of revenue resources in developing its global budget. The proposed level of Compact financial assistance in FY 2013 represents 37% of the total budget. A third of the Ministry's annual budget comes from two special revolving accounts allotted to the Ministry by law. The general fund contributes only 13%.

Surprisingly, both the proposed Compact base allocation and general fund amounts for the upcoming fiscal year *are lower than* the Ministry's actual appropriations in FY 2012. This situation would be untenable were it not for slightly increased special revenue allotments, more discretionary Federal grant funding and help from other external sources. Continued reliance on the latter two streams to shore up the Ministry's annual budget, however, is a dangerous practice. It not only will weaken maintenance of effort but it ultimately will undermine health improvements sought by the Ministry.

General funds and Compact financial assistance are the Ministry's only two flexible resources. The remaining budgetary inputs have predetermined uses. Because the Compact's annual decrements are unavoidable and will erode in terms of real value in the future, it behooves the Ministry to maintain fiscal discipline, raise fees for service where appropriate, and institute efficiency and effectiveness measures within its authority. These steps are essential to counteract declining funding for health.

General fund appropriations must step up to fill critical financial gaps and so too must political support be constant to sustain a sector capable of maintaining and improving the health of Marshallese citizens.

### The FY 2013 JEMFAC Request

Shown below is the Ministry of Health's request and proposed allocation of Compact funds by organizational performance area:

| | Area of Performance | Base Compact | ESN |
|---|---|---|---|
| Outcome 1 | Majuro Primary Care and Outer Islands Services | $1,251,246 | - |
| Outcome 2 | Majuro Hospital and Medical Referrals | $2,646,999 | - |
| Outcome 3 | Kwajalein Atoll: Ebeye Hospital | $772,423 | $1,410,557 |
| Outcome 4 | Kwajalein Atoll: Preventive Health Services | $305,963 | $347,078 |
| Outcome 5 | Administration and Finance | $1,717,139 | - |
| Outcome 6 | Health Information System | - | - |
| | **Total** | **$6,693,770** | **$1,757,635** |

The FY 2013 budget complies with *JEMFAC Resolution 2012-MT-1* that required the Ministry not to exceed its FY 2011 personnel-related expense level.

The budget also complied with *JEMFAC Resolution 2012-MT-4* that directed adequate funding for leprosy elimination, TB prevention and control, and the reduction of diabetes-related hospitalizations.

TB Initiative
| | |
|---|---|
| General Fund | $ 52,191 |
| Base Compact | $185,341 |
| Federal Grants | $ 94,887 |
| Health Care Revenue Fund | $150,000 |
| Global Fund | $ 88,000 |
| TOTAL | $570,419 |

Planning enabled continued vigilance and emphasis on Direct Observed Therapy (DOT). Upgrades have been finished to isolation wards at Majuro and Ebeye Hospitals. Expensive secondary drugs are now available at no cost from the World Health Organization. (RMI had seven accumulated MDR TB cases from 2009-2012. The goals are to reduce mortality and morbidity from TB by 10% and achieve zero new cases of MDR TB.)

Leprosy Elimination

| | |
|---|---|
| Base Compact | $146,192 |
| Health Fund | $121,500 |
| TOTAL | $267,692 |

The budget and activity plan enable continued emphasis on improved identification and follow-up of patients and contacts. The World Health Organization will support training of core program staff and assist in evaluating program effectiveness. The Ministry's mobile teams will extend skills development in detection and patient management to health assistants. (The goals are to reduce the prevalence of the disease to 1/10,000 population by 2017 and achieve a 90% or better treatment success rate. The 2011 prevalence baseline was 22/10,000.)

Reduction of Diabetes-Related Hospitalizations

| | |
|---|---|
| General Fund | $ 95,881 |
| Base Compact | $ 8,707 |
| Federal Grants | $291,806 |
| Health Care Revenue Fund | $ 20,000 |
| World Health Organization | $ 20,000 |
| TOTAL | $436,394 |

The addition of an initiative to reduce diabetes-related hospitalizations is JEMFAC's third health directive. The Ministry's budget covers diabetes prevention and management, and hypertension. It is primarily U.S. Federal grant-supported. The centerpiece to reducing recurring diabetes-related hospitalizations is better communication and shared patient management planning between hospital and primary care/public health. Neither intervention is cost intensive. (The goals are to implement a comprehensive Chronic Disease Self Management Support Program to reduce diabetic complications and to reduce both diabetes-related hospitalizations and secondary complications by 5% annually.)

The FY 2013 budgets and plans are adequate. However, leprosy elimination, tuberculosis control and diabetes management should not depend on competitive grants and foreign assistance.

### Compact Funding in the Context of the Proposed MOH Global Budget

In combination, base Compact and ESN funds comprise approximately 37% or $8,451,405 of the Ministry of Health's proposed $22,629,335 global budget for FY 2013. U.S. Federal grants contribute $4,084,483 or an additional 17% to the total budget. (Noteworthy is the fact that the Federal share is 4% higher than RMI's local appropriation.)

Almost a third of the global budget comes from special accounts administered by the Ministry from Social Security health care contributions, fees, and other revenues, with uses mandated by law. Only the general fund, Compact base funding, and ESN are flexible revenues that the Ministry can shift around.

The following table shows the proposed uses of funding by source:

**ed FY 2013 Uses By Fund Source**

Legend:
- Development and capital Expenses
- Operating Expenses
- Personnel-related Expenses

X-axis categories: General Funds, Base Compact, ESN, Special Hlth Funds, U.S. Federal, Other Funds

Y-axis: $-, $1,000,000, $2,000,000, $3,000,000, $4,000,000, $5,000,000, $6,000,000, $7,000,000

## Personnel-Related Expenses and Compact Funding

Personnel-related expenses account for $10,648,354 or 47% of the Ministry's multi-resourced global budget. This overall proportion is not out of line for governments with direct responsibility for providing the full range of health care services. However, the feature that makes the RMI's budget of special significance to JEMFAC is that the largest share falls to the base Compact grant (49%). The addition of the ESN allocation to personnel pushes the percentage to over 50%. The Ministry charges leased housing, a contracted perquisite for expatriate health workers in Majuro, to the Compact. At $766,497, this cost accounts for nearly 15% of the Compact's total personnel share.

General funds cover only 24% of the Ministry's personnel-related expenses and U.S. Federal grants, 17%.

The primary use of Compact funds to pay salaries, differentials, and other personnel-related costs constrains JEMFAC's ability to affect program outcomes.

## MOH's Special Health Funds Cover Most Non-Personnel Operating Costs with a Singular Exception

The Ministry's three special accounts (Health Fund, Health Care Revenue Fund, and Special Fund) cover a whopping 54% of operating expenses, with the largest costs attributable to the purchase of medical supplies and pharmaceuticals, and to paying for inter-island and off-island medical referrals. U.S. Federal grants cover most remaining costs. There is one area, however, where Compact funding carries the heaviest burden and that is in paying for utilities.

Compact funding picks up 79% of the Ministry's total annual electricity cost. The base Compact grant will direct $950,642 and ESN another $600,000 for a combined total of $1,550,642 in FY 2013, an amount that raises the Compact's contribution by $200,000 over FY 2012. This and past increases in utility investments have resulted in the "crowding out" of other recurring needs such as housekeeping and facilities maintenance supplies, POL, interisland travel by mobile teams, and medical equipment. Still, the amount proposed is inadequate for FY 2013 and monthly payment shortfalls are predictable without aggressive steps to trim the bill. Despite a recent energy audit that touted thousands of dollars of potential savings, the Ministry can only do so much because it is hampered by an aging power-hungry hospital in Majuro and it plays host to heavy kilowatt usage by the Diabetes Wellness Clinic's profitable catering business.

Tertiary Care and Off-Island Referrals

By operational necessity, the RMI's two 24-7 general hospitals on Majuro and Ebeye are costly enterprises. They employ most of the Ministry personnel and house patients who are chronically sicker than is typical at comparable facilities. It is a mistake, however, to assume that in-country hospital care is responsible for directing budgetary attention away from prevention and primary care.

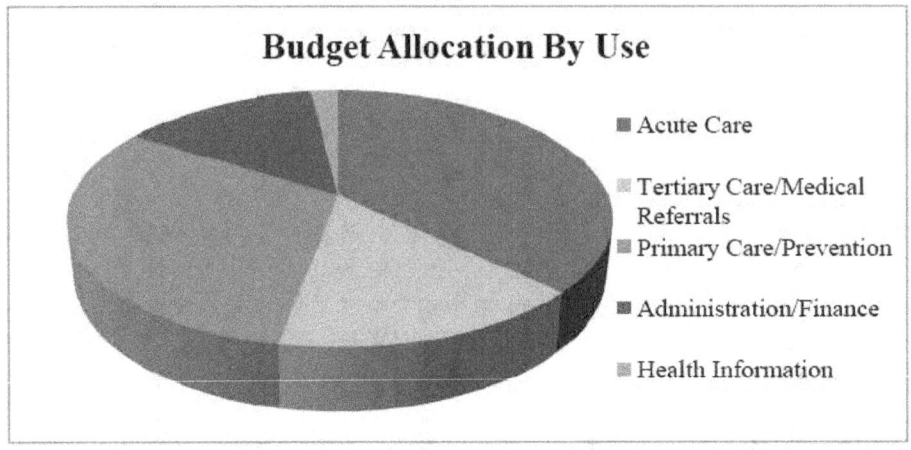

The pie chart above shows that the Ministry will spend $8,406,548 or 37% of its FY 2013 budget on on-island hospital care. A smaller but still respectable amount ($7,015,094 or 31%), will go to prevention and primary care.

At $3,586,998, costly out-of-country referrals will consume nearly one in five dollars of the FY 2013 global budget. This outflow of dollars represents a clear and present danger to the Ministry's ability to manage future budgetary declines, and undermines the use of funding, allowable by RMI law, to build the internal capacity needed to handle some common causes of referrals to the Philippines and Honolulu.

### Budget Inadequacy and Management Discipline

The Ministry of Health does not have adequate financial resources to achieve its strategic outcomes. Were it not for a sizeable and thus far sustained jump in fund allotments from "all others" in 2011, the Ministry would be in the midst of a severe crisis instead of waging a year-by-year struggle to maintain the status quo.

Base grant funding will drop in FY 2013 to $6,693,770 and there is every reason to believe the downturn in funding will be a constant until FY 2023, the last year of Compact grant assistance. Although ESN funding to the RMI increases in FY 2014, there is no assurance that health will continue to be a top priority for Kwajalein Atoll. If more money does go to hospital and preventive services, personnel and other recurring costs currently supported by the base Compact grant likely will shift to ESN to stabilize Majuro-centered operations.

Health care financing cannot stay static in the face of rising inflationary costs and the RMI's growing population of the young and the old who are higher risks for ill health. The saving's grace in the MOH's budget balancing act thus far has been the growth in "other funds," particularly in special health account allocations and U.S. Federal grant awards. However, as noted earlier, these sources have prescribed uses only. There also is not certainty that funding levels will remain stable over time.

In FY 2013, the Ministry will implement activities to counteract declining Compact dollars but realistically can only undertake those steps that are within its circumscribed management authority. Management discipline will be critical to that effort in the years that follow. The Ministry's senior administrators actively need to seek operating efficiencies. Programs with limited effectiveness should face elimination or consolidation.

Fee increases, changes in medical referral practices, transferring personnel from Compact to general funds, and the like require the prior consent of the RMI Executive Cabinet, the approval of the Nitijela, and unwavering political will for championing reforms. While conventional wisdom points to an infusion of general funds as a necessary corollary to maintaining and even circumspectly growing affordable health care of good quality, the future amount of general funding that will come to the Ministry is an unknown. What is apparent is that the amount will decrease in FY 2013.

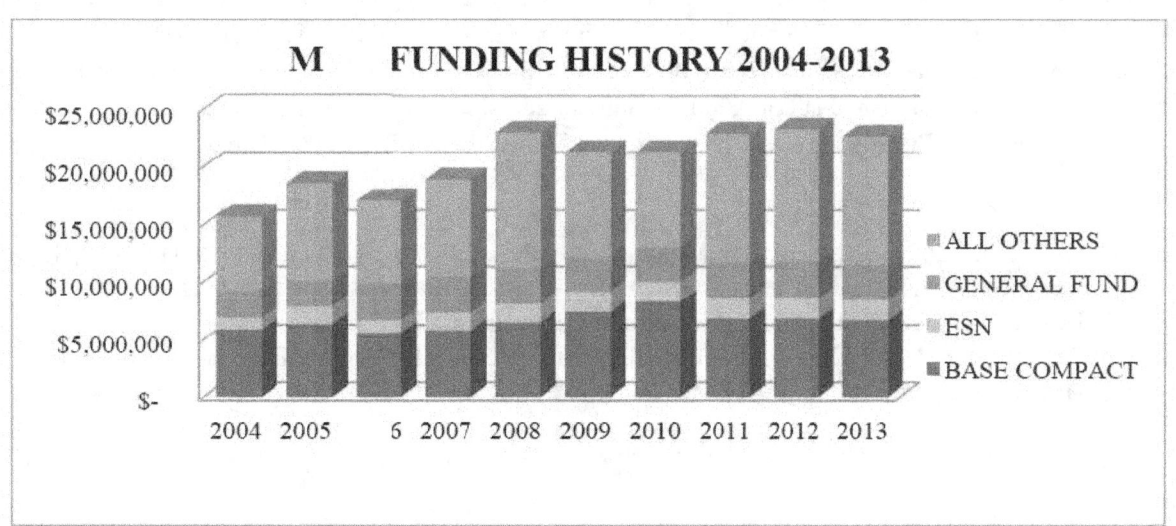

<u>Public Infrastructure</u>
The RMI allocated approximately $9.4 million for infrastructure improvements and maintenance in 2013. The RMI consistently adheres with the Amended Compacts' policy that at least 30% of all annual United

States Compact financial assistance made available through Section 211 of the Amended Compact be directed toward infrastructure development. To guide project selection, the RMI continued to utilize a comprehensive Infrastructure Development and Maintenance Program (IDMP) with complete project descriptions, timelines, financial requirements and measurable project indicators.

Projects funded during FY2013 are as follows:

> Ministry of Education Schools - $5,876,891
> Ministry of Health Capital Projects - $1,000,000
> Program Management Unit Operations - $400,000
> Preventive Maintenance- College of the Marshall Islands - $280,000
> Preventive Maintenance - Majuro Schools - $600,000
> Preventive Maintenance - Outer Island Schools - $800,000
> Preventive Maintenance - Majuro and Ebeye Hospitals - $250,000
> Preventive Maintenance- Outer Island Health Dispensaries - $200,000

Environment

In 2013, the RMI received an allocation of $231,420 for Kwajalein Environmental Impact. This amount is used to support the RMI Environmental Protection Agency (EPA) activities and programs on Ebeye. The RMI also received $325,000 to support capital needs for the Majuro Atoll Waste Corporation.

iii. **Fiscal Year 2013 Judicial Training Program**

Section 105(i)(1) of Public Law 108-188 established an annual program for the training of judges and officials of the judiciary in the Federated States of Micronesia and the Republic of the Marshall Islands in cooperation with the Pacific Islands Committee of the Ninth Circuit Judicial Council. The base amount of the program was established at $300,000, an amount adjusted annually by Section 118 of the Compact of Free Association. The 2013 program funding level is estimated at $353,000. The goals of the program are to:

- Train judges to provide fair, impartial and speedy justice, with a bench imbued with integrity, professionalism and competence.
- Train court leaders with ethical principles to train court staff.
- Train lawyers to provide a pool of qualified candidates to fill future judicial vacancies.
- Train court interpreters to provide access to justice in local communities.

5.

| Account: | Compact of Free Association (Permanent and Indefinite) | | | | | |
|---|---|---|---|---|---|---|
| **Activity:** | **Compact Impact   $(000)** | | | | | |
| | | | **2014** | | | |
| | *2013 Full Yr. CR (PL 112-175)* | **2012 Enacted** | Fixed Costs & Related Changes (+/-) | Program Changes (+/-) | Budget Request | Change from 2012 (+/-) |
| Hawaii | *11,210* | 11,229 | 0 | 0 | 11,229 | 0 |
| Guam | *16,799* | 16,827 | 0 | 0 | 16,827 | 0 |
| CNMI | *1,927* | 1,930 | 0 | 0 | 1,930 | 0 |
| American Samoa | *14* | 14 | 0 | 0 | 14 | 0 |
| Census | *50* | 0 | 0 | 0 | 0 | 0 |
| Total | *30,000* | 30,000 | **0** | **0** | **30,000** | **0** |
| FTEs | *0* | 0 | 0 | 0 | 0 | 0 |

## 2014 PROGRAM PERFORMANCE

The following 2013 grants will be made to each eligible jurisdiction based on the population of qualified migrants:

- Hawaii:                    $11,210,027
- Guam:                      $16,798,981
- CNMI:                      $ 1,927,228
- American Samoa:        $      13,764

Compact Impact grant assistance may be used only for health, educational, social, or public safety services, or infrastructure related to such services, specifically affected by qualified nonimmigrants. Each jurisdiction is to provide a spending plan to the Office of Insular Affairs (OIA) for the use of the funds prior to the awarding of the grant. The 2013 spending plans follow:

The State of Hawaii is expected to use the full 2013 amount of its $11.2 million to supplement state funds to support indigent health care as in past years.

Guam has proposed to use its 2013 Compact Impact grant of $16.8 million in the following manner:

- DPW Schools Leaseback                                          $7,100,000
- GMHA Operations Offset                                         $6,000,000
- GPD Operations Offset                                          $2,850,000
- DPW School Bus Satellite Facilities- Renovations        $ 350,000
- DISID Individualized Budget Program                       $ 200,000
- BSP Centralized Data Center Project                        $ 300,000

CNMI has proposed to use its 2013 Compact Impact grant of $1.9 million in the following manner:

- Department of Public Health                      $ 779,000
- Division of Youth Services                        $   50,000
- Department of Public Safety                      $ 515,000
- Department of Corrections                        $ 185,000
- Office of Public Defender                         $   27,000
- Northern Mariana College                        $ 167,000
- Public School System                        $   177,000

Although OIA has not yet received a 2013 spending plan for American Samoa, it is anticipated the funds will be used in a manner similar to 2012. The 2012 Compact Impact funding in the amount of $13,789 was used for the operational needs of the Nursing Program at the American Samoa Community College. The bulk of the funding was used for training materials and equipment to assist in the education of nursing students at the college.

6.

| Account: | Compact of Free Association (Permanent and Indefinite) | | | | | |
| --- | --- | --- | --- | --- | --- | --- |
| Activity: | Economic Assistance | | | | | |
| Subactivity: | Republic of Palau Compact $(000) | | | | | |

| | *2013 Full Yr. CR (PL 112-175)* | 2012 Enacted | 2014 | | | Inc (+) Dec(-) From 2012 |
| --- | --- | --- | --- | --- | --- | --- |
| | | | Fixed Costs & Related Changes (+/-) | Program Changes (+/-) | Budget Request | |
| Palau Compact* | 0 | 0 | 0 | +66,412 | 66,412 | +66,412 |
| FTEs | 0 | 0 | 0 | 0 | 0 | 0 |

\* Republic of Palau Legislative Proposal

## SUMMARY OF 2014 PROGRAM CHANGES

| Request Component | | |
| --- | --- | --- |
| Program Changes | Amount | FTE |
| Palau Compact | +66,412 | 0 |

## JUSTIFICATION OF 2014 PROGRAM CHANGES

The 2014 budget request includes $66.4 million and 0 FTE in recognition of the recently completed review of the relationship between the United States (U.S.) and the Republic of Palau (ROP). The results of the review were introduced by the U.S. Senate as S. 343.

## PROGRAM OVERVIEW

On February 14, 2011, S. 343 was introduced in the Senate seeking to continue the U.S. Compact financial relationship with the Republic of Palau. The proposed bill would provide $250 million in financial assistance to the Republic of Palau through 2024. The bill has not been enacted by the U.S. Congress to date. The goals of the continued funding are to maintain the viability of Palau's trust fund and to keep government spending stable while Palau enacts policy reforms to strengthen its economy.

Page Intentionally Blank

# Miscellaneous Schedules

# IV.  Miscellaneous Schedules

| 01085140412  0 | ==)ACCT_ID | | | |
| Assistance to Territories | ==)ACCT_TITLE | | | |
| PB2014 | ==)EXERCISE_NAME | | | |
| MASTER | ==)VERSION_NAME | | | |
| 2013-02-2621.44.01 | ==)LAST_UPDATE_DATE | | | |

| Line Title | Line | 2011 Act | 2012 Act | 2013 CY | 2014 BY |
|---|---|---|---|---|---|
| Combined Schedule (X) | | | | | |
| Obligations by program activity: | | | | | |
| Office of Insular Affairs | 0009 | | 12 | 10 | 9 |
| Technical assistance | 0010 | | 23 | 14 | 17 |
| Coral reef initiative | 0015 | | 1 | 1 | 1 |
| Water and wastewater projects | 0016 | | 1 | 1 | 0 |
| Maintenance assistance fund | 0017 | | 2 | 2 | 1 |
| American Samoa operations grants | 0018 | | 22 | 23 | 23 |
| Brown Treesnake | 0019 | | 3 | 3 | 4 |
| Empowering Insular Communities | 0021 | | 2 | 2 | 3 |
| Compact Impact Discretionary | 0031 | | 0 | 5 | 3 |
| Direct subtotal, discretionary | 0091 | | 66 | 61 | 61 |
| Covenant grants, mandatory | 0101 | | 33 | 28 | 28 |
| Total new obligations | 0900 | | 99 | 89 | 89 |
| | | | | | |
| Budgetary Resources: | | | | | |
| | | | | | |
| Unobligated balance: | | | | | |
| Unobligated balance brought forward, Oct 1 | 1000 | | 9 | 3 | 3 |
| Discretionary unobligated balance brought forward, Oct | 1001 | | 2 | 2 | |
| Recoveries of prior year unpaid obligations | 1021 | | 5 | 0 | 0 |
| Unobligated balance (total) | 1050 | | 14 | 3 | 3 |
| | | | | | |
| Budget authority: | | | | | |
| | | | | | |
| Appropriations, discretionary: | | | | | |
| Appropriation | 1100 | | 60 | 61 | 61 |
| Appropriation, discretionary (total) | 1160 | | 60 | 61 | 61 |
| Appropriation, discretionary - Computed Totals | 1160-20 | | 60 | 61 | 61 |
| | | | | | |
| Discretionary, Appropriations Committee | | | | | |
| Appropriation [Text] **OL Rates** | 1160-40 | | 60 | 61 | 61 |
| Baseline Non-Pay | 1160-50 | | 0 | 56 | 57 |
| Baseline Civilian Pay | 1160-50 | | 0 | 5 | 5 |
| Policy Outlays: | | | | | |
| New Authority | 1160-61 | | 50 | 40 | 40 |
| Balances (excl of EOY PY Bal) | 1160-62 | | 4 | 0 | 15 |
| End of PY Balances | 1160-63 | | 0 | 2 | 17 |
| Subtotal, outlays | 1160-64 | | 54 | 42 | 72 |
| Baseline Outlays: | | | | | |
| New Authority | 1160-81 | | 0 | 40 | 40 |
| Balances (excl of EOY PY Bal) | 1160-82 | | 0 | 0 | 15 |
| End of PY Balances | 1160-83 | | 0 | 2 | 17 |
| Subtotal, outlays | 1160-84 | | 0 | 42 | 72 |
| | | | | | |
| Appropriations, mandatory: | | | | | |
| Appropriation | 1200 | | 28 | 28 | 28 |
| Appropriations, mandatory (total) | 1260 | | 28 | 28 | 28 |
| Appropriations, mandatory - Computed Totals | 1260-20 | | 28 | 28 | 28 |

| | | | | |
|---|---|---|---|---|
| Mandatory, Authorizing Committee | | | | |
| Appropriation [Text] **OL Rates** | 1260-40 | 28 | 28 | 28 |
| Baseline Non-Pay | 1260-50 | 0 | 28 | 28 |
| Policy Outlays: | | | | |
| New Authority | 1260-61 | 21 | 1 | 1 |
| Balances (excl of EOY PY Bal) | 1260-62 | 0 | 0 | 7 |
| End of PY Balances | 1260-63 | 0 | 28 | 28 |
| Subtotal, outlays | 1260-64 | 21 | 29 | 36 |
| Baseline Outlays: | | | | |
| New Authority | 1260-81 | 0 | 1 | 1 |
| Balances (excl of EOY PY Bal) | 1260-82 | 0 | 0 | 7 |
| End of PY Balances | 1260-83 | 0 | 28 | 28 |
| Subtotal, outlays | 1260-84 | 0 | 29 | 36 |
| | | | | |
| Spending authority from offsetting collections, discretionary: | | | | |
| Spending auth from offsetting collections, disc (total) | 1750 | 0 | 0 | 0 |
| Budget authority (total) | 1900 | 88 | 89 | 89 |
| Total budgetary resources available | 1930 | 102 | 92 | 92 |
| | | | | |
| Memorandum (non-add) entries: | | | | |
| Unexpired unobligated balance, end of year | 1941 | 3 | 3 | 3 |
| | | | | |
| Change in obligated balance: | | | | |
| Unpaid obligations: | | | | |
| Unpaid obligations, brought forward, Oct 1 | 3000 | 159 | 180 | 198 |
| Obligations incurred, unexpired accounts | 3010 | 99 | 89 | 89 |
| Obligations incurred, expired accounts | 3011 | 2 | 0 | 0 |
| Outlays (gross) | 3020 | -75 | -71 | -108 |
| Recoveries of prior year unpaid obligations, unexpired | 3040 | -5 | 0 | 0 |
| | | | | |
| Unpaid obligations, end of year | 3050 | 180 | 198 | 179 |
| | | | | |
| Uncollected payments: | | | | |
| Uncollected pymts, Fed sources, brought forward, Oct | 3060 | -3 | -3 | -3 |
| Uncollected pymts, Fed sources, end of year | 3090 | -3 | -3 | -3 |
| | | | | |
| Memorandum (non-add) entries: | | | | |
| Obligated balance, start of year | 3100 | 156 | 177 | 195 |
| Obligated balance, end of year | 3200 | 177 | 195 | 176 |
| | | | | |
| Budget authority and outlays, net: | | | | |
| Discretionary: | | | | |
| Budget authority, gross | 4000 | 60 | 61 | 61 |
| Outlays, gross: | | | | |
| Outlays from new discretionary authority | 4010 | 50 | 40 | 40 |
| Outlays from discretionary balances | 4011 | 4 | 2 | 32 |
| Outlays, gross (total) | 4020 | 54 | 42 | 72 |
| Budget authority, net (discretionary) | 4070 | 60 | 61 | 61 |
| Outlays, net (discretionary) | 4080 | 54 | 42 | 72 |
| | | | | |
| Mandatory: | | | | |
| Budget authority, gross | 4090 | 28 | 28 | 28 |
| Outlays, gross: | | | | |
| Outlays from new mandatory authority | 4100 | 21 | 1 | 1 |
| Outlays from mandatory balances | 4101 | 0 | 28 | 35 |
| Outlays, gross (total) | 4110 | 21 | 29 | 36 |
| Budget authority, net (mandatory) | 4160 | 28 | 28 | 28 |
| Outlays, net (mandatory) | 4170 | 21 | 29 | 36 |
| Budget authority, net (total) | 4180 | 88 | 89 | 89 |
| Outlays, net (total) | 4190 | 75 | 71 | 108 |

| Object Classification (O) | | | | |
|---|---|---|---|---|
| Direct obligations: | | | | |
| Personnel compensation: | | | | |
| Personnel compensation: Full-time permanent | 1111 | | 4 | 4 | 4 |
| Civilian personnel benefits | 1121 | | 1 | 1 | 1 |
| Travel and transportation of persons | 1210 | | 1 | 1 | 1 |
| Other services from non-Federal sources | 1252 | | 2 | 2 | 2 |
| Other goods and services from Federal sources | 1253 | | 17 | 3 | 4 |
| Grants, subsidies, and contributions | 1410 | | 74 | 78 | 77 |
| Total new obligations | 9999 | | 99 | 89 | 89 |

| | | | | | |
|---|---|---|---|---|---|
| 01085140415 0 | ==)ACCT_ID | | | | |
| Compact of Free Association | ==)ACCT_TITLE | | | | |
| PB2014 | ==)EXERCISE_NAME | | | | |
| MASTER | ==)VERSION_NAME | | | | |
| 2013-02-2821.32.01 | ==)LAST UPDATE DATE | | | | |

| Line Title | Line | 2011 Act | 2012 Act | 2013 CY | 2014 BY |
|---|---|---|---|---|---|
| **Combined Schedule (X)** | | | | | |
| **Obligations by program activity:** | | | | | |
| Federal services assistance | 0001 | | 3 | 3 | 3 |
| Palau Compact Extension, mandatory | 0101 | | 14 | 13 | 0 |
| Subtotal | 0192 | | 17 | 16 | 3 |
| Assistance to the Marshall Islands | 0201 | | 68 | 68 | 75 |
| Assistance to the Federated States of Micronesia | 0202 | | 98 | 107 | 109 |
| Assistance to the Republic of Palau | 0203 | | 7 | 0 | 0 |
| Compact Impact | 0204 | | 34 | 30 | 30 |
| Subtotal, permanent indefinite | 0291 | | 207 | 205 | 214 |
| Total direct obligations | 0799 | | 224 | 221 | 217 |
| Reimbursable program | 0801 | | 18 | 18 | 18 |
| Total new obligations | 0900 | | 242 | 239 | 235 |
| | | | | | |
| **Budgetary Resources:** | | | | | |
| | | | | | |
| **Unobligated balance:** | | | | | |
| Unobligated balance brought forward, Oct 1 | 1000 | | 82 | 91 | 117 |
| Discretionary unobligated balance brought forward, Oct | 1001 | | 1 | 1 | |
| Recoveries of prior year unpaid obligations | 1021 | | 13 | 13 | 0 |
| Unobligated balance (total) | 1050 | | 95 | 104 | 117 |
| | | | | | |
| **Budget authority:** | | | | | |
| | | | | | |
| **Appropriations, discretionary:** | | | | | |
| Appropriation | 1100 | | 3 | 16 | 3 |
| Appropriation, discretionary (total) | 1160 | | 3 | 16 | 3 |
| Appropriation, discretionary - Computed Totals | 1160-20 | | 3 | 16 | 3 |
| | | | | | |
| **Discretionary, Appropriations Committee** | | | | | |
| Appropriation [see below for $2m] **OL Rates** | 1160-40 | | 3 | 3 | 3 |
| Baseline Non-Pay | 1160-50 | | 0 | 3 | 3 |
| Policy Outlays: | | | | | |
| New Authority | 1160-61 | | 3 | 3 | 3 |
| Balances (excl of EOY PY Bal) | 1160-62 | | 19 | 0 | 0 |
| End of PY Balances | 1160-63 | | 0 | 1 | 0 |
| Subtotal, outlays | 1160-64 | | 22 | 4 | 3 |
| Baseline Outlays: | | | | | |
| New Authority | 1160-81 | | 0 | 3 | 3 |
| Balances (excl of EOY PY Bal) | 1160-82 | | 0 | 0 | 0 |
| End of PY Balances | 1160-83 | | 0 | 1 | 0 |
| Subtotal, outlays | 1160-84 | | 0 | 4 | 3 |
| | | | | | |
| **Discretionary, Discretionary Change in a Mandatory Program, Appropriations Committee** | | | | | |
| Appropriation [Palau] **OL Rates** | 1160-40 | | 0 | 13 | 0 |
| Baseline Non-Pay | 1160-50 | | 0 | 13 | 0 |
| Policy Outlays: | | | | | |
| New Authority | 1160-61 | | 0 | 13 | 0 |
| Balances (excl of EOY PY Bal) | 1160-62 | | 0 | 0 | 0 |
| End of PY Balances | 1160-63 | | 0 | 0 | 0 |
| Subtotal, outlays | 1160-64 | | 0 | 13 | 0 |
| Baseline Outlays: | | | | | |
| New Authority | 1160-81 | | 0 | 13 | 0 |
| Balances (excl of EOY PY Bal) | 1160-82 | | 0 | 0 | 0 |
| End of PY Balances | 1160-83 | | 0 | 0 | 0 |
| Subtotal, outlays | 1160-84 | | 0 | 13 | 0 |

| | | | | |
|---|---|---|---|---|
| Appropriations, mandatory: | | | | |
| Appropriation | 1200 | 217 | 218 | 215 |
| Appropriations, mandatory (total) | 1260 | 217 | 218 | 215 |
| Appropriations, mandatory - Computed Totals | 1260-20 | 217 | 218 | 215 |
| | | | | |
| Mandatory, Authorizing Committee | | | | |
| Appropriation [Text] **OL Rates** | 1260-40 | 217 | 218 | 215 |
| Baseline Non-Pay | 1260-50 | 0 | 218 | 215 |
| Policy Outlays: | | | | |
| New Authority | 1260-61 | 178 | 185 | 183 |
| Balances (excl of EOY PY Bal) | 1260-62 | 42 | 0 | 11 |
| End of PY Balances | 1260-63 | 0 | 49 | 21 |
| Subtotal, outlays | 1260-64 | 220 | 234 | 215 |
| Baseline Outlays: | | | | |
| New Authority | 1260-81 | 0 | 185 | 183 |
| Balances (excl of EOY PY Bal) | 1260-82 | 0 | 0 | 11 |
| End of PY Balances | 1260-83 | 0 | 49 | 21 |
| Subtotal, outlays | 1260-84 | 0 | 234 | 215 |
| | | | | |
| Spending authority from offsetting collections, discretionary: | | | | |
| Collected | 1700 | 0 | 18 | 18 |
| Change in uncollected payments, Federal sources | 1701 | 18 | 0 | 0 |
| Spending auth from offsetting collections, disc (total) | 1750 | 18 | 18 | 18 |
| Spending auth from offsetting collections, disc - Comp | 1750-20 | 18 | 18 | 18 |
| | | | | |
| Discretionary, Appropriations Committee | | | | |
| Spending authority from offsetting collections [Text] | 1750-40 | 18 | 18 | 18 |
| Baseline Program [Text] | 1750-50 | 0 | 18 | 18 |
| Policy Outlays: | | | | |
| New Authority | 1750-61 | 0 | 2 | 2 |
| Balances (excl of EOY PY Bal) | 1750-62 | 0 | 0 | 16 |
| End of PY Balances | 1750-63 | 0 | 16 | 0 |
| Subtotal, outlays | 1750-64 | 0 | 18 | 18 |
| Baseline Outlays: | | | | |
| New Authority | 1750-81 | 0 | 2 | 2 |
| Balances (excl of EOY PY Bal) | 1750-82 | 0 | 0 | 16 |
| End of PY Balances | 1750-83 | 0 | 16 | 0 |
| Subtotal, outlays | 1750-84 | 0 | 18 | 18 |
| Budget authority (total) | 1900 | 238 | 252 | 236 |
| Total budgetary resources available | 1930 | 333 | 356 | 353 |
| | | | | |
| Memorandum (non-add) entries: | | | | |
| Unexpired unobligated balance, end of year | 1941 | 91 | 117 | 118 |
| | | | | |
| Change in obligated balance: | | | | |
| Unpaid obligations: | | | | |
| Unpaid obligations, brought forward, Oct 1 | 3000 | 134 | 121 | 78 |
| Obligations incurred, unexpired accounts | 3010 | 242 | 239 | 235 |
| Outlays (gross) | 3020 | -242 | -269 | -236 |
| Recoveries of prior year unpaid obligations, unexpired | 3040 | -13 | -13 | 0 |
| | | | | |
| Unpaid obligations, end of year | 3050 | 121 | 78 | 77 |

| | | | | |
|---|---|---|---|---|
| Uncollected payments: | | | | |
| Uncollected pymts, Fed sources, brought forward, Oct | 3060 | -23 | -20 | -20 |
| Change in uncollected pymts, Fed sources, unexpired | 3070 | -18 | 0 | 0 |
| Change in uncollected pymts, Fed sources, expired | 3071 | 21 | 0 | 0 |
| Uncollected pymts, Fed sources, end of year | 3090 | -20 | -20 | -20 |
| | | | | |
| Memorandum (non-add) entries: | | | | |
| Obligated balance, start of year | 3100 | 111 | 101 | 58 |
| Obligated balance, end of year | 3200 | 101 | 58 | 57 |
| | | | | |
| Budget authority and outlays, net: | | | | |
| Discretionary: | | | | |
| Budget authority, gross | 4000 | 21 | 34 | 21 |
| Outlays, gross: | | | | |
| Outlays from new discretionary authority | 4010 | 3 | 18 | 5 |
| Outlays from discretionary balances | 4011 | 19 | 17 | 16 |
| Outlays, gross (total) | 4020 | 22 | 35 | 21 |
| | | | | |
| Offsets against gross budget authority and outlays: | | | | |
| Offsetting collections (collected) from: | | | | |
| | | | | |
| Federal sources | 4030 | -19 | -18 | -18 |
| Federal sources (total) | 4030-10 | -19 | -18 | -18 |
| | | | | |
| Discretionary, Appropriations Committee | | | | |
| Policy Program [Text] | 4030-41 | -19 | -18 | -18 |
| Baseline Program [Text] | 4030-71 | 0 | -18 | -18 |
| | | | | |
| Additional offsets against gross budget authority only: | | | | |
| | | | | |
| Change in uncollected pymts, Fed sources, unexpire | 4050 | -18 | 0 | 0 |
| | | | | |
| Discretionary, Appropriations Committee | | | | |
| Policy Program [Text] | 4050-41 | -18 | 0 | 0 |
| Baseline Program [Text] | 4050-71 | 0 | 0 | 0 |
| | | | | |
| Offsetting collections credited to expired accounts | 4052 | 19 | 0 | 0 |
| | | | | |
| Discretionary, Appropriations Committee | | | | |
| from Education | 4052-41 | 19 | 0 | 0 |
| from Education | 4052-71 | 0 | 0 | 0 |
| Additional offsets against budget authority only (total) | 4060 | 1 | 0 | 0 |
| Budget authority, net (discretionary) | 4070 | 3 | 16 | 3 |
| Outlays, net (discretionary) | 4080 | 3 | 17 | 3 |
| | | | | |
| Mandatory: | | | | |
| Budget authority, gross | 4090 | 217 | 218 | 215 |
| Outlays, gross: | | | | |
| Outlays from new mandatory authority | 4100 | 178 | 185 | 183 |
| Outlays from mandatory balances | 4101 | 42 | 49 | 32 |
| Outlays, gross (total) | 4110 | 220 | 234 | 215 |
| Budget authority, net (mandatory) | 4160 | 217 | 218 | 215 |
| Outlays, net (mandatory) | 4170 | 220 | 234 | 215 |
| Budget authority, net (total) | 4180 | 220 | 234 | 218 |
| Outlays, net (total) | 4190 | 223 | 251 | 218 |
| | | | | |
| Object Classification (O) | | | | |
| | | | | |
| Direct obligations: | | | | |
| Other goods and services from Federal sources | 1253 | 3 | 3 | 3 |
| Grants, subsidies, and contributions | 1410 | 221 | 219 | 214 |
| Subtotal, obligations, Direct obligations | 1990 | 224 | 222 | 217 |
| | | | | |
| Reimbursable obligations: | | | | |
| Reimbursable obligations: Grants, subsidies, and contribu | 2410 | 18 | 17 | 18 |
| Total new obligations | 9999 | 242 | 239 | 235 |

| 01085140418  0 | ==)ACCT_ID | | | | |
|---|---|---|---|---|---|
| Payments to the United States Territories, Fiscal Assista | ==)ACCT_TITLE | | | | |
| PB2014 | ==)EXERCISE_NAME | | | | |
| MASTER | ==)VERSION_NAME | | | | |
| 2013-02-1410.07.45 | ==)LAST_UPDATE_DATE | | | | |

| Line Title | Line | 2011 Act | 2012 Act | 2013 CY | 2014 BY |
|---|---|---|---|---|---|
| Combined Schedule (X) | | | | | |
| Obligations by program activity: | | | | | |
| Advance payments to Guam of estimated U.S. income | 0001 | | 57 | 57 | 57 |
| Advance payments to the Virgin Islands of estimated U. | 0002 | | 256 | 283 | 258 |
| Total new obligations (object class 41.0) | 0900 | | 313 | 340 | 315 |
| | | | | | |
| Budgetary Resources: | | | | | |
| | | | | | |
| Budget authority: | | | | | |
| | | | | | |
| Appropriations, mandatory: | | | | | |
| Appropriation | 1200 | | 313 | 340 | 315 |
| Appropriations, mandatory (total) | 1260 | | 313 | 340 | 315 |
| Appropriations, mandatory - Computed Totals | 1260-20 | | 313 | 340 | 315 |
| | | | | | |
| Mandatory, Authorizing Committee | | | | | |
| Appropriation [Text] **OL Rates** | 1260-40 | | 313 | 340 | 315 |
| Baseline Non-Pay | 1260-50 | | 0 | 340 | 315 |
| Policy Outlays: | | | | | |
| New Authority | 1260-61 | | 313 | 340 | 315 |
| Balances (excl of EOY PY Bal) | 1260-62 | | 0 | 0 | 0 |
| End of PY Balances | 1260-63 | | 0 | 0 | 0 |
| Subtotal, outlays | 1260-64 | | 313 | 340 | 315 |
| Baseline Outlays: | | | | | |
| New Authority | 1260-81 | | 0 | 340 | 315 |
| Balances (excl of EOY PY Bal) | 1260-82 | | 0 | 0 | 0 |
| End of PY Balances | 1260-83 | | 0 | 0 | 0 |
| Subtotal, outlays | 1260-84 | | 0 | 340 | 315 |
| Total budgetary resources available | 1930 | | 313 | 340 | 315 |
| | | | | | |
| Change in obligated balance: | | | | | |
| Unpaid obligations: | | | | | |
| Unpaid obligations, brought forward, Oct 1 | 3000 | | 0 | 0 | 0 |
| Obligations incurred, unexpired accounts | 3010 | | 313 | 340 | 315 |
| Outlays (gross) | 3020 | | -313 | -340 | -315 |
| | | | | | |
| Unpaid obligations, end of year | 3050 | | 0 | 0 | 0 |
| | | | | | |
| Memorandum (non-add) entries: | | | | | |
| Obligated balance, start of year | 3100 | | 0 | 0 | 0 |
| Obligated balance, end of year | 3200 | | 0 | 0 | 0 |
| | | | | | |
| Budget authority and outlays, net: | | | | | |
| | | | | | |
| Mandatory: | | | | | |
| Budget authority, gross | 4090 | | 313 | 340 | 315 |
| Outlays, gross: | | | | | |
| Outlays from new mandatory authority | 4100 | | 313 | 340 | 315 |
| Budget authority, net (mandatory) | 4160 | | 313 | 340 | 315 |
| Outlays, net (mandatory) | 4170 | | 313 | 340 | 315 |
| Budget authority, net (total) | 4180 | | 313 | 340 | 315 |
| Outlays, net (total) | 4190 | | 313 | 340 | 315 |
| | | | | | |
| Object Classification (O) | | | | | |
| | | | | | |
| Direct obligations: | | | | | |
| Direct obligations: Grants, subsidies, and contributions | 1410 | | 313 | 340 | 315 |

| | |
|---|---|
| 01085144163 0 | ==)ACCT_ID |
| Assistance to American Samoa Direct Loan Financing Ac | ==)ACCT TITLE |
| PB2014 | ==)EXERCISE_NAME |
| MASTER | ==)VERSION NAME |
| 2013-02-0711.46.11 | ==)LAST UPDATE DATE |

| Line Title | Line | 2011 Act | 2012 Act | 2013 CY | 2014 BY |
|---|---|---|---|---|---|
| **Combined Schedule (X)** | | | | | |
| Obligations by program activity: | | | | | |
| Credit program obligations: | | | | | |
| Payment of interest to Treasury | 0713 | | 1 | 1 | 1 |
| Total new obligations | 0900 | | 1 | 1 | 1 |
| | | | | | |
| Budgetary Resources: | | | | | |
| | | | | | |
| Financing authority: | | | | | |
| | | | | | |
| Borrowing authority, mandatory: | | | | | |
| Borrowing authority, mandatory (total) | 1440 | | 0 | 0 | 0 |
| | | | | | |
| Spending authority from offsetting collections, mandatory: | | | | | |
| Collected | 1800 | | 2 | 2 | 2 |
| Spending authority from offsetting collections applied | 1825 | | -1 | -1 | -1 |
| Spending auth from offsetting collections, mand (total) | 1850 | | 1 | 1 | 1 |
| Financing authority (total) | 1900 | | 1 | 1 | 1 |
| Total budgetary resources available | 1930 | | 1 | 1 | 1 |
| | | | | | |
| Change in obligated balance: | | | | | |
| Unpaid obligations: | | | | | |
| Unpaid obligations, brought forward, Oct 1 | 3000 | | 0 | 0 | 1 |
| Obligations incurred, unexpired accounts | 3010 | | 1 | 1 | 1 |
| Financing disbursements (gross) | 3020 | | -1 | 0 | 0 |
| | | | | | |
| Unpaid obligations, end of year | 3050 | | 0 | 1 | 2 |
| | | | | | |
| Memorandum (non-add) entries: | | | | | |
| Obligated balance, start of year | 3100 | | 0 | 0 | 1 |
| Obligated balance, end of year | 3200 | | 0 | 1 | 2 |
| | | | | | |
| Financing authority and disbursements, net: | | | | | |
| | | | | | |
| Mandatory: | | | | | |
| Financing authority, gross | 4090 | | 1 | 1 | 1 |
| Financing disbursements: | | | | | |
| Financing disbursements, gross | 4110 | | 1 | 0 | 0 |
| | | | | | |
| Offsets against gross financing authority and disbursements: | | | | | |
| Offsetting collections (collected) from: | | | | | |
| | | | | | |
| Non-Federal sources - interest payments fr. Am. Sam | 4123 | | -2 | -1 | -1 |
| | | | | | |
| Non-Federal sources Principal Repayment American | 4123 | | 0 | -1 | -1 |
| Non-Federal sources (total) | 4123-10 | | -2 | -2 | -2 |
| Offsets against gross financing auth and disbursement | 4130 | | -2 | -2 | -2 |
| Financing authority, net (mandatory) | 4160 | | -1 | -1 | -1 |
| Financing disbursements, net (mandatory) | 4170 | | -1 | -2 | -2 |
| Financing authority, net (total) | 4180 | | -1 | -1 | -1 |
| Financing disbursements, net (total) | 4190 | | -1 | -2 | -2 |

| | | | | | |
|---|---|---|---|---|---|
| 01085140414  0 | ==)ACCT ID | | | | |
| Trust Territory of the Pacific Islands | ==)ACCT TITLE | | | | |
| PB2014 | ==)EXERCISE NAME | | | | |
| MASTER | ==)VERSION NAME | | | | |
| 2013-02-0710.26.27 | ==)LAST UPDATE DATE | | | | |

| Line Title | Line | 2011 Act | 2012 Act | 2013 CY | 2014 BY |
|---|---|---|---|---|---|
| Combined Schedule (X) | | | | | |
| Obligations by program activity: | | | | | |
| Technical Assistance | 0001 | | 1 | 0 | 0 |
| Total new obligations (object class 25.3) | 0900 | | 1 | 0 | 0 |
| | | | | | |
| Budgetary Resources: | | | | | |
| | | | | | |
| Unobligated balance: | | | | | |
| Unobligated balance brought forward, Oct 1 | 1000 | | 1 | 0 | 0 |
| | | | | | |
| Budget authority: | | | | | |
| | | | | | |
| Appropriations, discretionary: | | | | | |
| Appropriation, discretionary (total) | 1160 | | 0 | 0 | 0 |
| Appropriation, discretionary - Computed Totals | 1160-20 | | 0 | 0 | 0 |
| | | | | | |
| Discretionary, Appropriations Committee | | | | | |
| Appropriation [Text] | 1160-40 | | 0 | 0 | 0 |
| Baseline Civilian Pay | 1160-50 | | 0 | 0 | 0 |
| Policy Outlays: | | | | | |
| New Authority | 1160-61 | | 0 | 0 | 0 |
| Balances (excl of EOY PY Bal) | 1160-62 | | 1 | 0 | 0 |
| End of PY Balances | 1160-63 | | 0 | 0 | 0 |
| Subtotal, outlays | 1160-64 | | 1 | 0 | 0 |
| Baseline Outlays: | | | | | |
| New Authority | 1160-81 | | 0 | 0 | 0 |
| Balances (excl of EOY PY Bal) | 1160-82 | | 0 | 0 | 0 |
| End of PY Balances | 1160-83 | | 0 | 0 | 0 |
| Subtotal, outlays | 1160-84 | | 0 | 0 | 0 |
| Total budgetary resources available | 1930 | | 1 | 0 | 0 |
| | | | | | |
| Change in obligated balance: | | | | | |
| Unpaid obligations: | | | | | |
| Unpaid obligations, brought forward, Oct 1 | 3000 | | 2 | 2 | 2 |
| Obligations incurred, unexpired accounts | 3010 | | 1 | 0 | 0 |
| Outlays (gross) | 3020 | | -1 | 0 | 0 |
| | | | | | |
| Unpaid obligations, end of year | 3050 | | 2 | 2 | 2 |
| | | | | | |
| Memorandum (non-add) entries: | | | | | |
| Obligated balance, start of year | 3100 | | 2 | 2 | 2 |
| Obligated balance, end of year | 3200 | | 2 | 2 | 2 |
| | | | | | |
| Budget authority and outlays, net: | | | | | |
| Discretionary: | | | | | |
| Outlays, gross: | | | | | |
| Outlays from discretionary balances | 4011 | | 1 | 0 | 0 |
| Outlays, net (discretionary) | 4080 | | 1 | 0 | 0 |
| Budget authority, net (total) | 4180 | | 0 | 0 | 0 |
| Outlays, net (total) | 4190 | | 1 | 0 | 0 |
| | | | | | |
| Object Classification (O) | | | | | |
| | | | | | |
| Direct obligations: | | | | | |
| Direct obligations: Other goods and services from Federa | 1253 | | 1 | 0 | 0 |

Historical Table

**U.S. DEPARTMENT OF THE INTERIOR**
**OFFICE OF INSULAR AFFAIRS**
**COMPACT OF FREE ASSOCIATION (P.L. 99-239)**
**MARSHALL ISLANDS AND FEDERATED STATES OF MICRONESIA**
Estimated Payments 1987 - 2003
$'S In 000$

| | FY 1987 | FY 1988 | FY 1989 | FY 1990 | FY 1991 | FY 1992 | FY 1993 | FY 1994 | FY 1995 | FY 1996 | FY 1997 | FY 1998 | FY 1999 | FY 2000 | FY 2001 | TOTALS | FY 2002 | FY 2003 |
|---|---|---|---|---|---|---|---|---|---|---|---|---|---|---|---|---|---|---|
| **Republic of Marshall Islands (RMI)** | | | | | | | | | | | | | | | | | | |
| S 211 Capital and Current | 26,100 | 26,100 | 26,100 | 26,100 | 26,100 | 22,100 | 22,460 | 22,460 | 22,100 | 22,100 | 19,100 | 19,100 | 19,100 | 19,100 | 19,100 | 337,220 | 22,433 | 22,433 |
| S 217 Inflation | 6,468 | 6,816 | 7,668 | 8,520 | 9,656 | 9,272 | 10,004 | 10,736 | 11,224 | 11,712 | 10,700 | 11,342 | 11,342 | 11,556 | 11,984 | 149,000 | 14,384 | 14,384 |
| S 213 Kwajalein Impact | 1,900 | 1,900 | 1,900 | 1,900 | 1,900 | 1,900 | 1,900 | 1,900 | 1,900 | 1,900 | 1,900 | 1,900 | 1,900 | 1,900 | 1,900 | 28,500 | 1,900 | 1,900 |
| S 214 Energy Production | 0 | 2,000 | 2,000 | 2,000 | 2,000 | 2,000 | 2,000 | 2,000 | 2,000 | 2,000 | 2,000 | 2,000 | 2,000 | 2,000 | 2,000 | 28,000 | 1,867 | 1,867 |
| S 215 Communications O&M | 300 | 2,000 | 0 | 2,000 | 0 | 0 | 0 | 0 | 0 | 0 | 0 | 0 | 0 | 0 | 0 | 4,300 | 0 | 0 |
| S 215 Communications Hardware | 3,000 | 300 | 300 | 300 | 300 | 300 | 300 | 300 | 300 | 300 | 300 | 300 | 300 | 300 | 300 | 7,200 | 300 | 300 |
| S 111 Tax & Trade Compensation | 0 | 4,000 | 0 | 2,000 | 0 | 0 | 0 | 0 | 0 | 0 | 0 | 0 | 0 | 0 | 0 | 6,000 | 200 | 200 |
| S 216 Maritime Surveillance/Med Ref/Se | 2,367 | 1,700 | 1,700 | 1,700 | 1,700 | 1,700 | 1,700 | 1,700 | 1,700 | 1,700 | 1,700 | 1,700 | 1,700 | 1,700 | 1,700 | 26,167 | 1,744 | 1,744 |
| Subtotal | 40,135 | 44,816 | 39,668 | 44,520 | 41,656 | 37,272 | 38,364 | 39,096 | 39,224 | 39,712 | 35,700 | 36,342 | 36,342 | 36,556 | 36,984 | 586,387 | 42,828 | 42,828 |
| S 221 Health & Ed Block Grant | 3,000 | 3,000 | 3,000 | 3,000 | 3,000 | 3,000 | 3,000 | 3,000 | 3,000 | 3,000 | 3,000 | 3,000 | 3,000 | 3,000 | 3,000 | 45,000 | 3,000 | 3,000 |
| Military Use and Operating Rights G | 0 | 0 | 0 | 0 | 0 | 0 | 0 | 0 | 0 | 0 | 0 | 0 | 0 | 0 | 0 | 0 | 0 | 0 |
| Enewetak Operations | 900 | 1,100 | 1,100 | 1,100 | 1,094 | 1,094 | 1,091 | 1,091 | 1,089 | 1,091 | 1,091 | 1,191 | 1,576 | 1,191 | 1,388 | 17,187 | 1,391 | 1,620 |
| Rongelap Resettlement | 0 | 0 | 0 | 0 | 0 | 1,975 | 1,983 | 1,983 | 6,979 | 0 | 24,020 | 0 | 0 | 0 | 0 | 36,940 | 2,500 | 0 |
| Enjebi | 5,000 | 2,500 | 2,500 | 0 | 0 | 0 | 0 | 0 | 0 | 0 | 0 | 0 | 0 | 0 | 0 | 10,000 | 0 | 0 |
| Bikini Resettlement | 0 | 2,300 | 5,000 | 22,000 | 21,000 | 21,000 | 21,000 | 0 | 0 | 0 | 0 | 0 | 0 | 0 | 0 | 92,300 | 0 | 0 |
| Section 177 (Nuclear Claims) | 150,000 | 0 | 0 | 0 | 0 | 0 | 0 | 0 | 0 | 0 | 0 | 0 | 0 | 0 | 0 | 150,000 | 0 | 0 |
| Other Construction | 0 | 400 | 1,000 | 2,000 | 1,989 | 0 | 0 | 1,000 | 499 | 0 | 0 | 0 | 0 | 0 | 0 | 6,888 | 0 | 0 |
| **TOTAL - RMI** | 199,035 | 54,116 | 52,268 | 72,620 | 68,739 | 64,341 | 65,438 | 46,170 | 50,791 | 43,803 | 63,811 | 40,533 | 40,918 | 40,747 | 41,372 | 944,702 | 49,719 | 47,448 |
| **Federated States of Micronesia (FSM)** | | | | | | | | | | | | | | | | | | |
| S 211 Capital and Current | 60,000 | 60,000 | 60,000 | 60,000 | 60,000 | 51,000 | 51,000 | 51,000 | 51,000 | 51,000 | 40,000 | 40,000 | 40,000 | 40,000 | 40,000 | 755,000 | 50,333 | 50,333 |
| S 217 Inflation | 14,652 | 15,504 | 17,442 | 19,380 | 21,964 | 21,128 | 22,797 | 24,464 | 25,576 | 26,688 | 22,300 | 23,638 | 23,638 | 24,084 | 24,976 | 328,231 | 31,940 | 31,939 |
| S 214 Energy Production | 0 | 3,000 | 3,000 | 3,000 | 3,000 | 3,000 | 3,000 | 3,000 | 3,000 | 3,000 | 3,000 | 3,000 | 3,000 | 3,000 | 3,000 | 42,000 | 2,800 | 2,800 |
| S 215 Communications O&M | 600 | 600 | 600 | 600 | 600 | 600 | 600 | 600 | 600 | 600 | 600 | 600 | 600 | 600 | 600 | 9,000 | 600 | 600 |
| S 215 Communications Hardware | 6,000 | 0 | 0 | 0 | 0 | 0 | 0 | 0 | 0 | 0 | 0 | 0 | 0 | 0 | 0 | 6,000 | 400 | 400 |
| S 213 Yap Impact | 160 | 12,000 | 0 | 8,000 | 0 | 0 | 0 | 0 | 0 | 0 | 0 | 0 | 0 | 0 | 0 | 20,160 | 11 | 11 |
| S 111 Tax & Trade Compensation | 0 | 0 | 0 | 0 | 0 | 0 | 0 | 0 | 0 | 0 | 0 | 0 | 0 | 0 | 0 | 0 | 0 | 0 |
| S 216 Maritime/Med Ref/Scholarships | 4,335 | 3,669 | 3,669 | 3,669 | 3,669 | 3,669 | 3,669 | 3,669 | 3,669 | 3,669 | 3,669 | 3,669 | 3,669 | 3,669 | 3,669 | 55,701 | 3,713 | 3,713 |
| S 212 Civic Action Teams | 0 | 1,000 | 1,000 | 1,000 | 1,000 | 1,000 | 1,000 | 1,000 | 1,000 | 1,000 | 1,000 | 1,000 | 1,000 | 1,000 | 1,000 | 14,000 | 933 | 933 |
| Other Construction | 0 | 0 | 0 | 0 | 3,979 | 3,950 | 0 | 500 | 1,497 | 0 | 0 | 0 | 0 | 0 | 0 | 9,926 | 0 | 0 |
| Subtotal, permanent (FSM) | 85,747 | 95,773 | 85,711 | 95,649 | 94,212 | 84,347 | 82,066 | 84,233 | 86,342 | 85,957 | 70,569 | 71,907 | 71,907 | 72,353 | 73,245 | 1,240,018 | 90,730 | 90,729 |
| S 221 Health & Ed Block Grant | 7,000 | 7,000 | 7,000 | 7,000 | 7,000 | 7,000 | 7,000 | 7,000 | 7,000 | 7,000 | 7,000 | 7,000 | 7,000 | 7,000 | 7,000 | 105,000 | 7,000 | 7,000 |
| **TOTAL - FSM** | 92,747 | 102,773 | 92,711 | 102,649 | 101,212 | 91,347 | 89,066 | 91,233 | 93,342 | 92,957 | 77,569 | 78,907 | 78,907 | 79,353 | 80,245 | 1,345,018 | 97,730 | 97,729 |
| **Federal Services - FSM/RMI/Palau** | 18,750 | 17,320 | 12,760 | 10,160 | 7,660 | 7,810 | 7,294 | 7,528 | 6,514 | 6,964 | 6,964 | 7,354 | 7,354 | 7,120 | 7,338 | 138,890 | 7,354 | 7,306 |
| **GRAND TOTAL, RMI & FSM** | 310,532 | 174,209 | 157,739 | 185,429 | 177,611 | 163,498 | 161,798 | 144,931 | 150,647 | 143,724 | 148,344 | 126,794 | 127,179 | 127,220 | 128,955 | 2,428,610 | 154,803 | 152,483 |

## FSM-RMI Compact Payment Projections
### 2004-2008
*(in thousands of dollars)*

| | 2004 Base | 2004 Inflation 0.00% | 2004 Total | 2005 Base | 2005 Inflation 1.99% | 2005 Total | 2006 Base | 2006 Inflation 4.33% | 2006 Total | 2007 Base | 2007 Inflation 6.63% | 2007 Total | 2008 Base | 2008 Inflation 8.56% | 2008 Total | Subtotal 2004-2008 |
|---|---|---|---|---|---|---|---|---|---|---|---|---|---|---|---|---|
| **Federated States of Micronesia** | | | | | | | | | | | | | | | | |
| Annual Grant Section 211 | 76,200 | - | 76,200 | 76,200 | 1,514 | 77,714 | 76,200 | 3,296 | 79,496 | 75,400 | 5,002 | 80,402 | 74,600 | 6,387 | 80,987 | 394,800 |
| Audit Grant Section 212 (b) | 500 | - | 500 | 500 | - | 500 | 500 | - | 500 | 500 | - | 500 | 500 | - | 500 | 2,500 |
| Trust Fund Section 215 | 16,000 | - | 16,000 | 16,000 | 318 | 16,318 | 16,000 | 692 | 16,692 | 16,800 | 1,114 | 17,914 | 17,600 | 1,507 | 19,107 | 86,031 |
| *Total FSM Compact* | *92,700* | - | *92,700* | *92,700* | *1,832* | *94,532* | *92,700* | *3,988* | *96,688* | *92,700* | *6,116* | *98,816* | *92,700* | *7,894* | *100,594* | *483,331* |
| **Republic of the Marshall Islands** | | | | | | | | | | | | | | | | |
| Annual Grant Section 211 | 35,200 | - | 35,200 | 34,700 | 690 | 35,390 | 34,200 | 1,479 | 35,679 | 33,700 | 2,236 | 35,996 | 33,200 | 2,843 | 36,043 | 178,247 |
| Audit Grant Section 213 (b) | 500 | - | 500 | 500 | - | 500 | 500 | - | 500 | 500 | - | 500 | 500 | - | 500 | 2,500 |
| Trust Fund Section 216 (a&c) | 7,000 | - | 7,000 | 7,500 | 149 | 7,649 | 8,000 | 346 | 8,346 | 8,500 | 564 | 9,064 | 9,000 | 771 | 9,771 | 41,830 |
| Kwajalein Impact Section 212 | 15,000 | - | 15,000 | 15,000 | 298 | 15,298 | 15,000 | 649 | 15,649 | 15,000 | 995 | 15,995 | 15,000 | 1,284 | 16,284 | 78,226 |
| Rongelap Resettlement Section 103 (f)(4) | - | - | - | 1,780 | - | 1,780 | 1,760 | - | 1,760 | 1,760 | - | 1,760 | - | - | - | 5,300 |
| Enewetak Section 103 (f)(2)(c)(ii) | 1,300 | - | 1,300 | 1,300 | 26 | 1,326 | 1,300 | 56 | 1,356 | 1,300 | 86 | 1,386 | 1,300 | 111 | 1,411 | 6,780 |
| *Total RMI Compact* | *59,000* | - | *59,000* | *60,780* | *1,163* | *61,943* | *60,760* | *2,530* | *63,290* | *60,760* | *3,881* | *64,641* | *59,000* | *5,009* | *64,009* | *312,883* |
| **Compact-Other** | | | | | | | | | | | | | | | | |
| Compact Impact Section 104 (e) | 30,000 | - | 30,000 | 30,000 | - | 30,000 | 30,000 | - | 30,000 | 30,000 | - | 30,000 | 29,700 | (26) | 29,674 | 149,674 |
| Compact Impact Enumeration Section 104 (e)(4) | | | | | | | | | | | | | 300 | 26 | 326 | 326 |
| Judicial Training | 300 | - | 300 | 300 | 6 | 306 | 300 | 13 | 313 | 300 | 20 | 320 | 300 | 26 | 326 | 1,565 |
| *Total Compact-Other* | *30,300* | - | *30,300* | *30,300* | *6* | *30,306* | *30,300* | *13* | *30,313* | *30,300* | *20* | *30,320* | *30,300* | *26* | *30,326* | *151,565* |
| **GRAND TOTAL** | 182,000 | - | 182,000 | 183,780 | 3,001 | 186,781 | 183,760 | 6,532 | 190,292 | 183,760 | 10,017 | 193,777 | 182,000 | 12,929 | 194,929 | 947,778 |

## FSM-RMI Compact Payment Projections
### 2009-2013
*(in thousands of dollars)*

| | 2009 Base | 2009 Inflation 10.48% | 2009 Total | 2010 Base | 2010 Inflation 10.83% | 2010 Total | 2011 Base | 2011 Inflation 11.89% | 2011 Total | 2012 Base | 2012 Inflation 13.78% | 2012 Total | 2013 Base | 2013 Inflation 15.71% | 2013 Total | Subtotal 2009-2013 |
|---|---|---|---|---|---|---|---|---|---|---|---|---|---|---|---|---|
| **Federated States of Micronesia** | | | | | | | | | | | | | | | | |
| Annual Grant Section 211 | 73,800 | 7,732 | 81,532 | 73,000 | 7,904 | 80,904 | 72,200 | 8,582 | 80,782 | 71,400 | 9,839 | 81,239 | 70,600 | 11,092 | 81,691.50 | 406,147 |
| Audit Grant Section 212 (b) | 500 | - | 500 | 500 | - | 500 | 500 | - | 500 | 500 | - | 500 | 500 | - | 500.00 | 2,500 |
| Trust Fund Section 215 | 18,400 | 1,928 | 20,328 | 19,200 | 2,079 | 21,279 | 20,000 | 2,377 | 22,377 | 20,800 | 2,866 | 23,666 | 21,600 | 3,393 | 24,993.43 | 112,643 |
| *Total FSM Compact* | 92,700 | 9,659 | 102,359 | 92,700 | 9,983 | 102,683 | 92,700 | 10,959 | 103,659 | 92,700 | 12,705 | 105,405 | 92,700 | 14,485 | 107,185 | 521,291 |
| **Republic of the Marshall Islands** | | | | | | | | | | | | | | | | |
| Annual Grant Section 211 | 32,700 | 3,426 | 36,126 | 32,200 | 3,486 | 35,686 | 31,700 | 3,768 | 35,468 | 31,200 | 4,299 | 35,499 | 30,700 | 4,823 | 35,523 | 178,302 |
| Audit Grant Section 213 (b) | 500 | - | 500 | 500 | - | 500 | 500 | - | 500 | 500 | - | 500 | 500 | - | 500 | 2,500 |
| Trust Fund Section 216 (a&c) | 9,500 | 995 | 10,495 | 10,000 | 1,083 | 11,083 | 10,500 | 1,248 | 11,748 | 11,000 | 1,516 | 12,516 | 11,500 | 1,807 | 13,307 | 59,148 |
| Kwajalein Impact Section 212 | 15,000 | 1,571 | 16,571 | 15,000 | 1,624 | 16,624 | 15,000 | 1,783 | 16,783 | 15,000 | 2,067 | 17,067 | 15,000 | 2,357 | 17,356.552 | 84,402 |
| Rongelap Resettlement Section 103 (f)(4) | | | | | | | | | | | | | | | | |
| Enewetak Section 103 (f)(2)(c)(i) | 1,300 | 136 | 1,436 | 1,300 | 141 | 1,441 | 1,300 | 155 | 1,455 | 1,300 | 179 | 1,479 | 1,300 | 204 | 1,504 | 7,315 |
| *Total RMI Compact* | 59,000 | 6,129 | 65,129 | 59,000 | 6,334 | 65,334 | 59,000 | 6,953 | 65,953 | 59,000 | 8,061 | 67,061 | 59,000 | 9,191 | 68,191 | 331,668 |
| **Compact-Other** | | | | | | | | | | | | | | | | |
| Compact Impact Section 104 (e) | 30,000 | - | 30,000 | 30,000 | - | 30,000 | 30,000 | - | 30,000 | 30,000 | - | 30,000 | 29,700 | (47) | 29,653 | 149,653 |
| Compact Impact Enumeration Section 104 (e)(4) | | | | | | | | | | | | | 300 | 47 | 347 | 347 |
| Judicial Training | 300 | 31 | 331 | 300 | 32 | 332 | 300 | 36 | 336 | 300 | 41 | 341 | 300 | 47 | 347 | 1,688 |
| *Total Compact-Other* | 30,300 | 31 | 30,331 | 30,300 | 32 | 30,332 | 30,300 | 36 | 30,336 | 30,300 | 41 | 30,341 | 30,300 | 47 | 30,347 | 151,688 |
| **GRAND TOTAL** | 182,000 | 15,820 | 197,820 | 182,000 | 16,349 | 198,349 | 182,000 | 17,947 | 199,947 | 182,000 | 20,807 | 202,807 | 182,000 | 23,723 | 205,723 | 1,004,646 |

**FSM-RMI Compact Payment Projections**
**2014-2018**
*(in thousands of dollars)*

| | 2014 Base | 2014 Inflation 17.71% | 2014 Total | 2015 Base | 2015 Inflation 19.71% | 2015 Total | 2016 Base | 2016 Inflation 21.71% | 2016 Total | 2017 Base | 2017 Inflation 23.71% | 2017 Total | 2018 Base | 2018 Inflation 25.71% | 2018 Total | Subtotal 2014-2018 |
|---|---|---|---|---|---|---|---|---|---|---|---|---|---|---|---|---|
| **Federated States of Micronesia** | | | | | | | | | | | | | | | | |
| Annual Grant Section 211 | 69,800 | 12,362 | 82,162 | 69,000 | 13,600 | 82,600 | 68,200 | 14,806 | 83,006 | 67,400 | 15,981 | 83,381 | 66,600 | 17,123 | 83,723 | 414,872 |
| Audit Grant Section 212 (b) | 500 | - | 500 | 500 | - | 500 | 500 | - | 500 | 500 | - | 500 | 500 | - | 500 | 2,500 |
| Trust Fund Section 215 | 22,400 | 3,967 | 26,367 | 23,200 | 4,573 | 27,773 | 24,000 | 5,210 | 29,210 | 24,800 | 5,880 | 30,680 | 25,600 | 6,582 | 32,182 | 146,212 |
| *Total FSM Compact* | 92,700 | 16,329 | 109,029 | 92,700 | 18,173 | 110,873 | 92,700 | 20,017 | 112,717 | 92,700 | 21,861 | 114,561 | 92,700 | 23,705 | 116,405 | 563,585 |
| **Republic of the Marshall Islands** | | | | | | | | | | | | | | | | |
| Annual Grant Section 211 | 32,200 | 5,703 | 37,903 | 31,700 | 6,248 | 37,948 | 31,200 | 6,774 | 37,974 | 30,700 | 7,279 | 37,979 | 30,200 | 7,765 | 37,965 | 189,768 |
| Audit Grant Section 213 (b) | 500 | - | 500 | 500 | - | 500 | 500 | - | 500 | 500 | - | 500 | 500 | - | 500 | 2,500 |
| Trust Fund Section 216 (a&c) | 12,000 | 2,125 | 14,125 | 12,500 | 2,464 | 14,964 | 13,000 | 2,822 | 15,822 | 13,500 | 3,201 | 16,701 | 14,000 | 3,599 | 17,599 | 79,212 |
| Kwajalein Impact Section 212 | 18,000 | 3,188 | 21,188 | 18,000 | 3,548 | 21,548 | 18,000 | 3,908 | 21,908 | 18,000 | 4,268 | 22,268 | 18,000 | 4,628 | 22,628 | 109,539 |
| Rongelap Resettlement Section 103 (f)(4) | - | - | - | - | - | - | - | - | - | - | - | - | - | - | - | - |
| Enewetak Section 103 (f)(2)(c)(i) | 1,300 | 230 | 1,530 | 1,300 | 256 | 1,556 | 1,300 | 282 | 1,582 | 1,300 | 308 | 1,608 | 1,300 | 334 | 1,634 | 7,911 |
| *Total RMI Compact* | 64,000 | 11,246 | 75,246 | 64,000 | 12,516 | 76,516 | 64,000 | 13,786 | 77,786 | 64,000 | 15,056 | 79,056 | 64,000 | 16,326 | 80,326 | 388,930 |
| **Compact-Other** | | | | | | | | | | | | | | | | |
| Compact Impact Section 104 (e) | 30,000 | - | 30,000 | 30,000 | - | 30,000 | 30,000 | - | 30,000 | 30,000 | - | 30,000 | 29,700 | (77) | 29,623 | 149,623 |
| Compact Impact Enumeration Section 104(e)(4) | - | - | - | - | - | - | - | - | - | - | - | - | 300 | 77 | 377 | 377 |
| Judicial Training | 300 | 53 | 353 | 300 | 59 | 359 | 300 | 65 | 365 | 300 | 71 | 371 | 300 | 77 | 377 | 1,826 |
| *Total Compact-Other* | 30,300 | 53 | 30,353 | 30,300 | 59 | 30,359 | 30,300 | 65 | 30,365 | 30,300 | 71 | 30,371 | 30,300 | 77 | 30,377 | 151,826 |
| **GRAND TOTAL** | 187,000 | 27,628 | 214,628 | 187,000 | 30,748 | 217,748 | 187,000 | 33,868 | 220,868 | 187,000 | 36,988 | 223,988 | 187,000 | 40,108 | 227,108 | 1,104,341 |

## FSM-RMI Compact Payment Projections
### 2019-2023
*(in thousands of dollars)*

| | 2019 Base | 2019 Inflation 27.71% | 2019 Total | 2020 Base | 2020 Inflation 29.71% | 2020 Total | 2021 Base | 2021 Inflation 31.71% | 2021 Total | 2022 Base | 2022 Inflation 33.71% | 2022 Total | 2023 Base | 2023 Inflation 35.71% | 2023 Total | Subtotal 2019-2023 | Total 2004-2023 |
|---|---|---|---|---|---|---|---|---|---|---|---|---|---|---|---|---|---|
| **Federated States of Micronesia** | | | | | | | | | | | | | | | | | |
| Annual Grant Section 211 | 65,800 | 18,233 | 84,033 | 65,000 | 19,312 | 84,312 | 64,200 | 20,358 | 84,558 | 63,400 | 21,372 | 84,772 | 62,600 | 22,355 | 84,955 | 422,630 | 1,638,449 |
| Audit Grant Section 212 (b) | 500 | - | 500 | 500 | - | 500 | 500 | - | 500 | 500 | - | 500 | 500 | - | 500 | 2,500 | 10,000 |
| Trust Fund Section 215 | 26,400 | 7,316 | 33,716 | 27,200 | 8,081 | 35,281 | 28,000 | 8,879 | 36,879 | 28,800 | 9,709 | 38,509 | 29,600 | 10,570 | 40,170 | 184,554 | 529,442 |
| *Total FSM Compact* | *92,700* | *25,549* | *118,249* | *92,700* | *27,393* | *120,093* | *92,700* | *29,237* | *121,937* | *92,700* | *31,081* | *123,781* | *92,700* | *32,925* | *125,625* | *609,685* | *2,177,891* |
| **Republic of the Marshall Islands** | | | | | | | | | | | | | | | | | |
| Annual Grant Section 211 | 29,700 | 8,230 | 37,930 | 29,200 | 8,675 | 37,875 | 28,700 | 9,101 | 37,801 | 28,200 | 9,506 | 37,706 | 27,700 | 9,892 | 37,592 | 188,904 | 735,222 |
| Audit Grant Section 213 (b) | 500 | - | 500 | 500 | - | 500 | 500 | - | 500 | 500 | - | 500 | 500 | - | 500 | 2,500 | 10,000 |
| Trust Fund Section 216 (a&c) | 14,500 | 4,018 | 18,518 | 15,000 | 4,457 | 19,457 | 15,500 | 4,915 | 20,415 | 16,000 | 5,394 | 21,394 | 16,500 | 5,892 | 22,392 | 102,176 | 282,365 |
| Kwajalein Impact Section 212 | 18,000 | 4,988 | 22,988 | 18,000 | 5,348 | 23,348 | 18,000 | 5,708 | 23,708 | 18,000 | 6,068 | 24,068 | 18,000 | 6,428 | 24,428 | 118,539 | 390,707 |
| Rongelap Resettlement Section 103 (f)(4) | - | - | - | - | - | - | - | - | - | - | - | - | - | - | - | - | 5,300 |
| Enewetak Section 103(f)(2)(c)(i) | 1,300 | 360 | 1,660 | 1,300 | 386 | 1,686 | 1,300 | 412 | 1,712 | 1,300 | 438 | 1,738 | 1,300 | 464 | 1,764 | 8,561 | 30,567 |
| *Total RMI Compact* | *64,000* | *17,596* | *81,596* | *64,000* | *18,866* | *82,866* | *64,000* | *20,136* | *84,136* | *64,000* | *21,406* | *85,406* | *64,000* | *22,676* | *86,676* | *420,680* | *1,454,161* |
| **Compact-Other** | | | | | | | | | | | | | | | | | |
| Compact Impact Section 104 (e) | 30,000 | - | 30,000 | 30,000 | - | 30,000 | 30,000 | - | 30,000 | 30,000 | - | 30,000 | 29,700 | (107) | 29,593 | 149,593 | 598,543 |
| Compact Impact Enumeration Section 104 (e)(4) | - | - | - | - | - | - | - | - | - | - | - | - | 300 | 107 | 407 | 407 | 1,457 |
| Judicial Training | 300 | 83 | 383 | 300 | 89 | 389 | 300 | 95 | 395 | 300 | 101 | 401 | 300 | 107 | 407 | 1,976 | 7,054 |
| *Total Compact-Other* | *30,300* | *83* | *30,383* | *30,300* | *89* | *30,389* | *30,300* | *95* | *30,395* | *30,300* | *101* | *30,401* | *30,300* | *107* | *30,407* | *151,976* | *607,054* |
| **GRAND TOTAL** | 187,000 | 43,228 | 230,228 | 187,000 | 46,348 | 233,348 | 187,000 | 49,468 | 236,468 | 187,000 | 52,588 | 239,588 | 187,000 | 55,708 | 242,708 | 1,182,341 | 4,239,106 |

U.S. DEPARTMENT OF THE INTERIOR
OFFICE OF INSULAR AFFAIRS
COMPACT OF FREE ASSOCIATION
REPUBLIC OF PALAU
Budget Authority 1995 - 2009
$'S IN 000'S

| ACTIVITY (P.L. 99-658) | FY 1995 | FY 1996 | FY 1997 | FY 1998 | FY 1999 | FY 2000 | FY 2001 | FY 2002 | FY 2003 | FY 2004 | FY 2005 | FY 2006 | FY 2007 | FY 2008 | FY 2009 | TOTALS |
|---|---|---|---|---|---|---|---|---|---|---|---|---|---|---|---|---|
| Sect 211(a) Current Account | 12,000 | 12,000 | 12,000 | 12,000 | 7,000 | 7,000 | 7,000 | 7,000 | 7,000 | 7,000 | 6,000 | 6,000 | 6,000 | 6,000 | 6,000 | 120,000 |
| Sect 211(b) Energy Production | 28,000 | | | | | | | | | | | | | | | 28,000 |
| Sect 211(c) Communications | 1,650 | 150 | 150 | 150 | 150 | 150 | 150 | 150 | 150 | 150 | 150 | 150 | 150 | 150 | 150 | 3,750 |
| Sect 211(d) Maritime Surveillance, Health, Scholarships | 631 | 631 | 631 | 631 | 631 | 631 | 631 | 631 | 631 | 631 | 631 | 631 | 631 | 631 | 631 | 9,465 |
| Sect 211(e) Start-up for 211(d) | 667 | | | | | | | | | | | | | | | 667 |
| Sect 211(f) Investment Fund a/ | 66,000 | | 4,000 | | | | | | | | | | | | | 70,000 |
| Subtotal Sec 211 | 108,948 | 12,781 | 16,781 | 12,781 | 7,781 | 7,781 | 7,781 | 7,781 | 7,781 | 7,781 | 6,781 | 6,781 | 6,781 | 6,781 | 6,781 | 231,882 |
| Sect 212(b) Capital Account | 36,000 | | | | | | | | | | | | | | | 36,000 |
| Sect 213 Defense Use Impact | 5,500 | | | | | | | | | | | | | | | 5,500 |
| Sect 215 Inflation Adjustment | 35,719 | 5,842 | 6,075 | 6,440 | 3,790 | 3,861 | 4,004 | 4,076 | 4,290 | 4,362 | 3,875 | 3,998 | 4,121 | 4,244 | 4,367 | 99,060 |
| SUBTOTAL | 186,167 | 18,623 | 22,856 | 19,221 | 11,571 | 11,642 | 11,785 | 11,857 | 12,071 | 12,143 | 10,656 | 10,779 | 10,902 | 11,025 | 11,148 | 372,442 |
| Sect 221(b) Special Block Grant | 6,300 | 4,900 | 3,500 | 2,000 | 2,000 | 2,000 | 2,000 | 2,000 | 2,000 | 2,000 | 2,000 | 2,000 | 2,000 | 2,000 | 2,000 | 38,700 |
| DIRECT PAYMENTS | 192,467 | 23,523 | 26,356 | 21,221 | 13,571 | 13,642 | 13,785 | 13,857 | 14,071 | 14,143 | 12,656 | 12,779 | 12,902 | 13,025 | 13,148 | 411,142 |
| Federal Services | 1,340 | 0 | 0 | 0 | 0 | 0 | 0 | 1,539 | 1,539 | 1,539 | 1,539 | 1,539 | 1,539 | 1,539 | 1,539 | 13,652 |
| Sect 212(a) Palau Road Construction | 53,000 | 0 | 96,000 | 0 | 0 | 0 | 0 | | | | | | | | | 149,000 |
| GRAND TOTAL, PALAU | 246,807 | 23,523 | 122,356 | 21,221 | 13,571 | 13,642 | 13,785 | 15,396 | 15,610 | 15,682 | 14,195 | 14,318 | 14,441 | 14,564 | 14,687 | 573,794 |

a/ PALAU MAY WITHDRAW $5 MILLION ANNUALLY FROM THE FUND IN YEARS 5 THROUGH 15

**Estimated Payments 2010-2024**

**$'S IN 000'S**

| Sec | ACTIVITY (Revised Agreement) | FY 2010 | FY 2011 | FY 2012 | FY 2013 | FY 2014 | FY 2015 | FY 2016 | FY 2017 | FY 2018 | FY 2019 | FY 2020 | FY 2021 | FY 2022 | FY 2023 | FY 2024 | TOTALS 1/ |
|---|---|---|---|---|---|---|---|---|---|---|---|---|---|---|---|---|---|
| 1 | Trust Fund Contributions | | | | | 6,000 | 8,000 | 3,000 | 3,000 | 2,000 | 2,000 | 2,000 | 2,000 | 2,000 | 250 | 0 | 30,250 |
| 2a | Infrastructure Maintenance Fund 2/ | | | | | 6,912 | 2,000 | 2,000 | 2,000 | 2,000 | 2,000 | 2,000 | 2,000 | 2,000 | 2,000 | 2,000 | 26,912 |
| 3 | Fiscal Consolidation Fund - Discretionary | | | | | | | | | | | | | | | | 0 |
| | Fiscal Consolidation Fund - Mandatory | | | | | 10,000 | | | | | | | | | | | 10,000 |
| 4a | Economic Assistance - Discretionary | 13,147 | 13,147 | 13,147 | 13,147 | | | | | | | | | | | | 52,588 |
| | Economic Assistance - Mandatory | | | | | 12,000 | 11,500 | 10,000 | 8,500 | 7,250 | 6,000 | 5,000 | 4,000 | 3,000 | 2,000 | | 69,250 |
| 5 | Infrastructure Projects | | | | | 30,000 | 5,000 | 5,000 | | | | | | | | | 40,000 |
| | *Direct Assistance to Palau - Discretionary* | *13,147* | *13,147* | *13,147* | *13,147* | | | | | | | | | | | | *52,588* |
| | **Direct Assistance to Palau - Mandatory** | | | | 0 | 64,912 | 26,500 | 20,000 | 13,500 | 11,250 | 10,000 | 9,000 | 8,000 | 7,000 | 4,250 | 2,000 | 176,412 |
| | Total, Direct Assistance to Palau | 13,147 | 13,147 | 13,147 | 13,147 | 64,912 | 26,500 | 20,000 | 13,500 | 11,250 | 10,000 | 9,000 | 8,000 | 7,000 | 4,250 | 2,000 | 229,000 |
| | Postal Service Subsidy | | | | | 1,500 | 1,500 | 1,500 | 1,500 | 1,500 | 1,500 | 1,500 | 1,500 | 1,500 | 1,500 | 1,500 | 16,500 |
| | ANNUAL FUNDING, PALAU COMPACT | 13,147 | 13,147 | 13,147 | 13,147 | 66,412 | 28,000 | 21,500 | 15,000 | 12,750 | 11,500 | 10,500 | 9,500 | 8,500 | 5,750 | 3,500 | 245,500 |
| | PALAU ANNUAL WITHDRAWAL FROM TRUST FUND 3/ | 5,000 | 5,000 | 5,000 | 5,000 | 5,250 | 5,500 | 6,750 | 8,000 | 9,000 | 10,000 | 10,500 | 11,000 | 12,000 | 13,000 | 15,000 | 126,000 |

1/ Discretionary appropriations provided by the Congress in 2010-2013 italicized

2/ Entry Into Force repayment (Sec 212) $3 million paid into Infrastructure Maintenance Fund

3/ Palau is limited by agreement from withdrawing more than this amount from its US-funded Compact Trust Fund

www.ingramcontent.com/pod-product-compliance
Lightning Source LLC
Chambersburg PA
CBHW081103290526
45795CB00006B/1972